THE CRITICS ROAR WITH LAUGHTER

"Jack Douglas has been keeping America laughing since 1938 with comedy material for such entertainers as Bob Hope, Phil Harris, Red Skelton, and Eve Arden. He has written many hilarious books, and he has done it again."

San Francisco *Examiner*

"I read WHAT DO YOU HEAR FROM WALDEN POND? while in the hospital. It was a good place to be because I was sick from laughing."

Johnny Carson

"Jack Douglas is a different kind of man—a very funny one. He is not just a writer, but a comedy writer, and one of the best in America."

Chicago *Sun Times*

"Jack Douglas has picked up the sputtering torch of American written humor that once glowed so brightly and was carried so proudly by so many before the deluge of radio and television doused it into a flickering ember."

Variety

Also by Jack Douglas

Where better paperbacks are sold, or directly from the pub-
lisher. Include 15¢ per copy for mailing; allow three weeks for
delivery.

Avon Books, Mail Order Dept., 250 West 55th Street,
New York, N. Y. 10019

JACK DOUGLAS
WHAT DO YOU HEAR FROM WALDEN POND?

AVON
PUBLISHERS OF BARD, CAMELOT, DISCUS, EQUINOX AND FLARE BOOKS

AVON BOOKS
A division of
The Hearst Corporation
959 Eighth Avenue
New York, New York 10019

First Avon Printing, July, 1974.

To Henry David Thoreau, who said, "The spending of the best part of one's life earning money is a questionable pursuit."

And to J. Paul Getty, who said, "Huh?"

1

FOR two years, Reiko and I and our two sons, Bobby, who was eight years old, and two-year-old Timothy, whom we called our Ski-Doo baby because he was born on a snowmobile in a blizzard, had been living on Lost Lake in a magnificent hunting-fishing complex, deep in the wild Canadian bush country of northern Ontario.

For two years, we had battled snow, ice, black flies, wind, rain, uncertain transportation, an untrustworthy radiotelephone, a tricky electric generator, plus a thousand other unexpected backwoods contingencies, and we loved every minute of it.

But after two years, I began to have little pricks of conscience. Although Reiko seemed to like the big woods as much as I did, I wondered if she was just being sweet about the whole thing. She never saw anyone except a few merchants, in Chinookville—116 miles away where we did our shopping—and Mr. and Mrs. Trilby, our nearest neighbors, who lived in a tiny cabin on Starvation Lake, 60 miles to the east of us. We didn't see much of them because Mr. and Mrs. Trilby were very old. If something hadn't gone wrong in Mother Nature's scheme, they would have been fossilized and lying in an ancient stream bed, surrounded by diplodocus footprints, but instead, when they felt so inclined, they snowmobiled the 60 miles from Starvation Lake to Lost Lake in less than two hours to have dinner with us.

"That crazy son of a bitch," Sandra Trilby said between puffs of her omnipresent wet cigar, "drives like he's Barney Oldfield."

Lambert and Sandra Trilby were good neighbors (because they lived 60 miles from us), and Reiko was always very happy to see them, but I had the feeling that she would have been happier to see almost anyone else. The Trilbys were not the ideal dinner guests. No matter what especially nongaseous food Reiko prepared, Lambert and Sandra invariably broke wind after every third bite. Alternately. A stranger would have thought we were playing old bass fiddle solos on our hi-fi. As they had to tilt just before each blast, the effect was that of having dinner aboard a small boat on a rough sea. During a thunderstorm.

I also felt I was depriving Bobby of a normal boy's life. He had no friends except frogs, red squirrels, chipmunks, a beaver who thought he was one of the family, and our own animals: Tanuki, a Montana timber wolf, Pussycat, our female cougar, Chibi, the Malamute, and Doggie, the four-pound Pomeranian, plus a younger timber wolf. A large and interesting group, but none with which he could play kick ball. He tried it once with Tanuki and in less than one minute the kickball had been shredded by the wolf's enormous canine teeth.

At the same time, I knew in the back of my mind that his education was being neglected because I was his teacher. We had long ago abandoned the almost impossible trek across the lake and through the woods to the school bus stop—some 13 miles away. Toward the termination of this hopeless task, the school bus had been completely empty, which gave me some consolation—I wasn't the only loving father who got goddamn sick and tired of fighting snow, mud and fallen trees to make it out of the woods in time to catch the school bus at 7 A.M. on those black winter mornings, plus the prospect of doing the whole thing over, in reverse, when my child got off the bus, alone, in the five o'clock dark in the middle of the forest and waited for his father, who lived in fear of a vehicle (Land Rover or J-5 caterpillar or snowmobile) breakdown on his way to the remote bus stop. What would Bobby do, alone on that almost never traveled secondary road to nowhere? If I didn't meet him, would he be able to walk the 13 miles home through the dark woods? He couldn't have walked 50 feet if there had been snow during the day, and I never in a million years could have gone that distance, even with snowshoes, to meet him. This possibility alone made us all decide that *I* would teach him. Even if he never got past C-A-T spells C-A-T and 2 plus 2 equals whatever it equals, at least he would be alive and warm.

I probably used the excuse of Reiko's well of hidden loneliness and Bobby's sketchy crack at the world of education to erase whatever doubts I was having about the advisability of continuing to live apart from the human race, but still a strange change happened. Always in our cozy, octagon-shaped bedroom, with its floor-to-ceiling windows allowing the moonlight to search out every corner during its journey through the heavens, I had slept under a mountain of fire-red Hudson Bay Four-point blankets like a Beechnut-baby-food-filled baby, but there came a time when I became disturbed by dreams. Or I should say, a recurrent dream.

Every third night or so, I would dream about the Old Trapper. Every winter the Old Trapper journeyed into the deep wilderness to do his thing, which was trapping mink, beaver, marten, fisher and whatever else he could sell every year at the big North Bay fur auction. The Old Trapper did not own a watch or a clock. He spurned the offer of a free nudie calendar from the Chinookville garage. All he took with him as he snowmobiled back into the bush was a hundred pounds of flour, a few cans of baking soda, a couple of bottles of whiskey and an old Indian lady, who was his housekeeper. This old Indian lady was of indeterminate age, but any guess over ninety and under two hundred would have been approximately correct. She was withered and wrinkled beyond anything Charlie Revson could have done for her. The only clue that she was female was the Empress Eugénie hat she wore over her fur parka. She also had a brand-new pair of panty hose, with which she used to net salmon in the Wanapitei River. Those panty hose filled with live, floundering salmon looked like Juliet Prowse doing one of her best numbers.

When asked, by no one in particular, with no watch, no clock, and no calendar, how the Old Trapper knew when it was time to come out of the bush, he replied, "When that old Indian lady starts looking good to me."

This is a hoary old joke told around a thousand and one smoky campfires on long, lonely winter's nights, by hoary old trappers who think *they're* as funny as Johnny Carson any day, but it is on the ragged edge of serving to illustrate the way I was beginning to feel about our life in the northern Ontario bush.

Reiko always looked good to me, so I couldn't use her as a calendar. I really had no clear indication of what was becoming a slight hunger for life on the outside. When we lived in Old New Litchridge and other suburban Connecticut outposts, we hadn't felt the urge or need to mingle, except for an occasional trip to the bright lights of the A&P or some other fun spot, so it couldn't be that we were yearning to become, once again, part of the scene or be in a position where we could take the Old New Litchridge garden tour whenever we felt like it. There was something else that kept gnawing at what was left of my vitals. Maybe it *was* because of Bobby. His education, with me as his teacher, was as sporadic as Leontyne Price singing "O cieli azzurri" from *Aïda* with the hiccups. The emphasis was all in the wrong places. Bobby had learned how to locate the North Star. How to find his way back out of the forest when he was seemingly lost, and how to avoid mashing his skull against a jaywalking tree while snowmobiling through the bush. (This miracle is accomplished by body English and prayer.) And what to do if his nose turned white after a couple of hours out in 35-below-zero weather, but this was hardly the training he needed in order to get into a good computer school. How would it look on his application under "experience"? "I know what to do if my nose turns white—"

I really wasn't too worried about Bobby's education. If things didn't work out at Harvard, he could always get a mail-order priesthood and set up a church in an abandoned store and make a fortune selling Raquel Welch's bath water to Tibetan monks (they don't have television, you know).

Timothy, the baby, was too young to worry about his education. All he knew how to do at his age was to be happy. He giggled and gurgled from the time our pet wolves howled us into consciousness in the morning until they chorused a mournful taps at night.

Something else upset my tranquility and contentment among the murmuring pines and the hemlocks. I wanted to see the new Paris subway. I had read all about it in the Chinookville *Star*, where it was a page-one hot flash, although I don't know why. Not very many Chinookvillians ever went to Paris. Or anywhere else. They had an attitude, "Why go away when you're already here?" They may have had something, but it wasn't fascination with the outside world. I wanted to see the new Paris subway because, according to the Chinookville *Star*'s story, at one of its stations not only could you feed peanuts to a live elephant penned down there, but you could have a herring sandwich for three francs or your urine analyzed for the same price. A hard choice if all you had was three francs and you were hungry and you had any curiosity at all about your urine.

Paris had always had a strange mystique for me. I had been there with my mother in 1935 when everything was going on—Hemingway, Gertrude Stein, Colette, and all that—but being with my mother, we drank very little absinthe (which was the LSD of the thirties) and seldom bought any Modigliani paintings in exchange for a drink or a pinch of hashish. In fact, we didn't even know Modigliani—or if he was still around.

We *did* know Bernie Applefeld, who lived at our pension and who had been sent to Paris and the Sorbonne, by his mother, to learn how to be a certified public accountant—a course of study which was strangely missing from the Sorbonne's curricula (Bernie Applefeld subsequently learned)—so he had taken up sculpture instead and was sculpting, he confided to my mother and me one night, after a few beers, a statue of Mount Everest—life-size.

We didn't see much of Bernie Applefeld because with a

project like that he obviously had his work cut out for him.

Anyway, Bernie Applefeld didn't strike me as the type who would know any famous Parisians. He never went to the Dôme or the Deux Maggots or the Mort Rat. His idea of a big evening in Gay Paree was a Laurel and Hardy movie at the Cinéma Montparnasse, and a cup of cocoa, with a marshmallow in it, afterward. And I doubt if he ever knew any demimondaines, which was unfortunate for me because he was my only entrée to this kind of carry-ings-on. He did introduce me to a friend of his mother's once, but although this friend had long blond curls and bee-stung lips, I was quite sure that it was a boy. I was only eighteen at the time, so I wasn't much interested in boys yet.

Mother and I got loaded on muscatel one night and went to the Folies Bergère, so we had plenty to talk about when we got home, even though nobody in Far Rockaway believed us.

I was lying in the sun on our airplane dock, in the Canadian North, when my musings about those gay, care-free days in Paris were interrupted by a phone call from Beverly Hills, California—from an agent for whom I have had the utmost disrespect ever since I can remember.

"Hello, Jack!" boomed over our fifteen-party radio-phone. "How are things in the big north woods and wad-dya hear from Nelson Eddy?"

"He's dead," I said. "Who *is* this?"

"Clipper," the voice said, "Frank Clipper. I'm in Bev-erly Hills."

"Finally made it, eh?" I said.

"What?"

"Never mind," I said. "How are things in Beverly Hills?"

"Jumping! This is where you ought to be."

"I don't jump much anymore," I said. "I'm developing poise."

"How's that?" he said. "This connection is lousy—I seem to be getting cut off all the time."

"I'm talking on a radiophone," I said. "I have to press a button every time I want to talk. What's on your mind?"

"Johnny Blackwell," he said. "Johnny's crazy about you. He reads all your books and everything!" He sounded nervous. I remembered Frank Clipper from the old Hollywood days when he was elbowing his way—trying to find an opening in the ranks through which he could reach the top. At that time he had only two clients—an aging glamour girl who had had her bust lifted so many times she could have nursed a papoose, and an eager young juvenile who wanted to be another Conway Tearle. Frank Clipper had plenty of reasons to be nervous in those days—nervous that he wasn't going to make it. Evidently he had made it.

"I'm glad that Johnny Blackwell is crazy about me," I said. "And I think it's very kind of you to call me and tell me."

"He wants you," Clipper said.

"Huh?"

"He wants you to come out here to Hollywood and write a movie—a movie for television."

"That's funny," I said. "Every time I read anything about him it says that he doesn't use writers. He ad-libs his shows—that's why they're so spontaneous and funny."

"Well, yes," Clipper said. "He does an awful lot of ad-libbing, but he needs subjects—he needs somebody he can try things out on."

"He should become a Catholic," I said.

"What's that? This goddamn phone!"

"I said, why doesn't he join the Catholic church? Then he could go to confession and try out his routines and the priest could tell him what to do—or give him absolution or something."

"Oh—it's a joke," he said.

"Sort of," I said. This Frank Clipper has become a little sharper, but not much.

"Why don't you come out here, write the movie, and see if you like it? Bring your wife. We'll getcha a nice little house at the beach."

"I also have two kids, a Malamute, a Pomeranian, two wolves and a mountain lion."

"We'll get you a cage," he said. "How do you like Malibu?"

"You haven't mentioned money," I said.

"Jack," he almost whined, "you've got to *trust* me!" The last time I trusted him I had to spend three days in court trying to recover a whole season's salary because of a contract personally arranged by him. Since then I won't sign my name on a filling station washroom wall without a lawyer.

"I *do* trust you," I said. "Mention money." He mumbled for a few moments, then came up with a figure which was very flattering and would have bought a lot of improvements to our Lost Lake camp, but I knew that the first price wasn't always the best price.

"It costs a lot of money to live in California," I said.

"Look," he said, "Johnny's *crazy* about you."

"Yeah," I said, "and I'm crazy about him, but will the Chamber of Commerce of California lower the prices just because of *that?*"

"Jesus Christ," Frank Clipper said, "you always were a bastard to do business with!"

This was the old Frank Clipper that I knew. "Okay," I said, "give me the price that they authorized you to offer and let's cut out the shit!"

"Okay," he shouted, "cutting out the shit, they will pay you"—and he mentioned an even more flattering figure—"and your fare out here!"

"I'll think about it," I said and hung up. The phone rang almost immediately but I didn't answer it.

"How would you like to go to California?" I said.

"You mean to Disneyland?" Bobby said.

"I guess I do," I said. "But they used to call it California."

"I thought you didn't like it out there anymore," Reiko said.

"I don't," I said. "But we could use the money. Johnny Blackwell is going to make a movie."

"He's funny," Bobby said.

"Yeah." Timothy, who was now almost two years old, giggled.

"Timothy likes him," Reiko said.

"Yeah," I said, "Timothy also likes zwiebach."

"Who's zwiebach?" Bobby said.

"He's a doctor in Africa," Reiko said.

"That's Schweitzer," I said, "and he's dead."

"Oh," Reiko said.

"I know why he's dead," Bobby said. "He was bitten by a tsetse fly."

"That's not quite the whole story," I said, with a deep sense of guilt suddenly coming over me at the sad state of Bobby's education. It became clearer day by day that he would never be the proud possessor of a high school diploma. Or a grammar school diploma. He might pick up an honorary degree at some enfeebled nursery school, but that would be about it. I didn't know whether the California school system would be the answer, but at least he might learn that there were other creatures in the world besides beavers, bear and moose. Which was a good thing to know, if you were selling used cars or thinking about opening a fancy hi-colonic studio. Hi-colonics were very popular in California, along with human sacrifices and savings and loan associations, which amounted to the same thing.

The decision to leave the assured uncertainties of Lost Lake for the certified quicksands of Hollywood was very difficult. I was eaten by curiosity to find out if I could capture some of the old carefree spirit of California living, or maybe this was just a desire to live my life over again, which I knew was silly and impossible. I knew it would be like a veteran of World War I going back to that little village on the Marne expecting to find Renée Adoree or John Gilbert. I also knew I could not live my life over again. I've already done that three times before and made the same mistakes each time.

I knew if I went back to Hollywood and California I could not visit the places where I had spent twenty-five years of my life, such as the 22-acre ranch I had owned in the San Fernando Valley, which is now a state park and

very beautiful. Trees I had planted when they were only a
foot or two high had risen to 60 and 70 feet. There were
redwoods and Monterey pines, birch, and many other
varieties which I had skillfully blended for natural effects.
I had also built a fantastic cement block home with a lavish swimming pool and other luxurious appointments. All
this is still there, but across the road, what previously had
been a lovely 100-acre horse ranch was now a shopping
center, complete with liquor stores, five-and-dimes and a
car wash. All the beautiful leggy colts, and splendid mares,
stallions and geldings have disappeared into the never-
never land of wistful memories. I could never go back and
view this "progress" without a deep hurting sadness or a
seething rage.

But this was only part of my hang-up about the California scene. I was also afraid. This sounds very maudlin and
dreary, and idiotic, and it is, but I was scared to death to
return to Hollywood and meet one of the blond blue-eyed
starlets and semi-starlets I had been crazy about and discover she has transmogrified into a blob. Of course, she
may not be too thrilled that I'm not still Ricardo Cortez
either. Of course, some of the Golden Girls I knew still
look pretty good. Like Lucille Ball. I knew Lucille Ball
when I was a Busby Berkeley boy and she was a gorgeous
show girl. I'm sorry to say I never knew her intimately because if I had played my cards right, I might have completely eliminated that Cuban bongo player and that other
chap. I never would have met My Darling Reiko, but I
would have had an empire instead of a Japanese fortune
cookie.

There were two girls in Hollywood whom I was very
friendly with, but neither of them would have anything to
do with me physically. One, who would only date me in
the afternoon because she was going steady with a doctor.
I thought this would work out because Cyrano or Shake-
speare or maybe it was Georgie Jessel had counseled that
the best time to make out with a girl was just after the
sun was over the mast. Meaning that the clod who worked
all day was not in much of a position to guard his most
precious possession, while a wastrel, such as I seemed to

be because I did no work in the afternoon, would have a great chance to knock off anything floating around loose. But with this particular girl it didn't work out this way at all. She was faithful to that goddamn doctor and withstood every masculine wile I could cook up and my powers of invention were endless, but it was like landing on Omaha Beach with a water pistol. Not that I ever got as far as landing on the beach with her. She finally married the doctor. Strange how some girls will just ruin their chances.

The other unconquerable was and *is* probably the sexiest girl in the movies. She has only two rivals so far as femininity is concerned—Sophia Loren and Raquel Welch. Formidable competition, but not for this lovely. She had all the postures and titivating mannerisms of a wanton and the mind of a religious fanatic lesbian nun. She had been a dancer and, unlike most dancers, she had bosoms. There seems to be a limit, from all I've read, in describing this particular part of a woman's body and that's where I find myself at the moment. There is only one word that I can think of for this particular pair and that is "magnificent." She'll never need a brassiere. Her legs were long and her tiny waist curved her hips into exquisite proportions. She had absolutely the most perfect body and her mind matched it. She was brilliant. Maybe too brilliant. I never got anyplace with her either, and after a few years of trying, and quite a few professional separations, the whole thing dissolved into a few impersonal notes and "Good Luck" telegrams on opening nights. A sad commentary on the life of an apprentice satyr.

In my soul-searching of the pros and cons of returning to California, I thought of both of these lovely creatures, and in the back of my foolish mind I thought, "Gee— maybe—?" Which of course proves once again that writers are not just unstable—they're lunatics. Or maybe dreamers. Or just plain troublemakers—for themselves, anyway.

I was also a little worried about my reception in Hollywood in other directions. In my day out there, I had been sort of a minor king (or a major prince) of comedy writ-

ing. Everybody had known and loved me to some degree,
but I kept hearing (while in the bush) about the New
Hollywood and all the new people who were doing great
things. I wondered about these "new" people (until they
turned out to be all my old friends who had dignified their
first names—"Joe" became "Joseph," "Hank" became
"Henry," Herbie became "Herbert," and Mort became
"Morton J."), so I needn't have fretted on this point.

I pushed these aspects of a Hollywood sojourn from my
mind and tried to concentrate on other problems which
would surely come up if we made the move from the pris-
tine loveliness of the Canadian bush to the tired tinsel of
Peter Lawfordland. We would have to find an apartment
house that would welcome children, dogs, wolves and a
cougar. This didn't seem much of a problem because I had
never seen a sign on any Hollywood apartment reading NO
WOLVES, NO COUGARS. But I remembered there seemed
great antipathy toward children. Maybe a house would be
the thing, although people who had houses to rent were no
less tolerant of anything younger than eighteen and walking upright. This rather limited us and our menagerie, and
I hadn't walked upright too much lately, either. I didn't
dwell on the problem of housing too much; I knew that
the studio would come through with something if we put
up a large enough bond to guarantee that we wouldn't
walk on the carpets or sit in the chairs or use the
bathroom or the swimming pool or deface the walls by removing the owner's (usually a movie personality) thousand and one still shots of him (or her) taken during his
(or her) long career in the silents. A special agreement
also would have to be reached about the Spanish shawl on
the grand piano. Most Hollywood rental agreements about
this priceless accouterment insisted that it be left as is—
draped brocadedly across the top of the Steinway, its
years of accumulated dust to be left intact and unmolested,
with the silver-framed autographed pictures of H. B.
Warner, Ronald Colman and Slim Summerville posi-
tioned as they had always been since the millennium—or
bond would be forfeited.

But all this would not be my headache, I felt—if they

really wanted me out there. And if they really *want* you in Hollywood, you can get away with murder—as has happened more than once in that tight little community. If they *don't* want you, you can be arrested for loitering in your own bathtub.

For three days I thought about Frank Clipper's call from Hollywood. I took long, solitary walks in the forest, making sure to stick to the blaze-marked trail so I wouldn't lose my way—thinking all the time how much simpler life would be in the comfort and convenience of a conventional home. At least in Hollywood I wouldn't have to worry about getting lost. Or would I?

The northern Canadian forest land is beautiful in the spring. The new leaves of the white birches and the wisps of green of the tamaracks made a lacy scrim across the dark background of fir and spruce and pine. And it was quiet. I think it was during these three days of walking through this silent primeval cathedral I began, for the first time, to realize how quiet it was. Outside of an occasional Canada jay, there were very few birds in the woods. And no songbirds. The animals were there, but it was seldom that you ever caught a glimpse of them. The whole thing became a tomb. The silence was everywhere. Suddenly, I felt unnerved. I was alone in a terrible vacuum. The silence screaming all around me. Enveloping me.

I walked as fast as I could, stumbling over slippery rocks and half-rotted trees. I wanted to get home and turn on the radio. I wanted to hear something besides the pounding of my heart.

I had never experienced this in the woods before—or since—but I took it as a suggestion—or maybe a warning. *Get out of the woods—now!*

When I arrived back on our little home island, I said nothing to Reiko, but I wondered if she had ever had a traumatic shock like this, or maybe it was just me. Maybe I was going mad.

I wanted the advice of my ever-faithful (if he had nothing else to do) agent, Irving Laveeeene. (I had a hunch his name used to be Levine, but he changed it because he was so short—4 feet 11 in his stocking feet, and he reasoned that, being short, he would be better off with a tall name.) Irving was the best agent I had ever had, and although he had never gotten me a job, he was always on deck when some other agent came up with something. This was the way it was this time, too. Charlie Burke splashed his Cessna 180 down into Lost Lake one lovely June morning, and instead of a surprise packet of stacked-up mail, he delivered Irving Laveeeene. I couldn't believe it because Irving had spent a week with us some two years before and had become a gibbering lunatic from the remoteness and quiet.

"What the hell?" was the first thing I said as he tripped down the rungs of the Cessna, completely missing the bottom rung and inadvertently stepping with his hundred-dollar unborn suede shoes into the icy-cold waters of the lake.

"Jesus Christ!" Irving said. "This son of a bitchin' water is cold! Why the hell didn't you hole up in the Bahamas or some other place, where they got sense enough to have warm water?"

"I'd like to go somewhere where they have warm water," Reiko said, wistfully, I thought.

"I gotta use the phone," Irving said. "I told Peter Fonda I'd call him the minute I got here."

"I'm gonna call Jane Fonda the minute I get to Hollywood," I said. "I'm gonna tell her I'm an Indian and we Indians got a great idea—we're gonna give the United States back to the white man, and she'll have to get the hell out!"

"Very funny," Irving said, picking up his king-size attaché case.

"You gonna need me anymore, massa?" Charlie Burke asked.

"Another funny man," Irving said. "Yes, I'm gonna need you. Just wait."

"Yazzuh, massa," Charlie Burke said. "I'll leave the meter running."

Before I could ask since when did a bush plane have a meter, Irving started to hustle Reiko up the path to the lodge, followed by Bobby and Chibi, the Malamute, Doggie, the Pomeranian, and Tanuki, the wolf (the main lodge was on an island, so we could let him run loose). "Pretty mean-looking police dog," I could hear Irving say.

"That's a wolf," Bobby said.

"Jesus Christ!" Irving said. "I'm glad I'm not Little Bo-peep."

"That's Little Red Riding Hood," Bobby said.

"Which one?" Irving said.

"The one that got eaten by the wolf in that son of a bitchin' lying fairy story," Bobby said.

"You oughtta talk to that boy," Irving said to Reiko. "He's got his folklore all fucked up."

"Jack-san teaches him," Reiko said.

"That's like the monster teaching Frankenstein," Irving said. "Where's the phone?" By this time we had reached the lodge and Irving was puffing considerably from the short uphill trek from the airplane dock.

"You're in great shape," I said. "If we lived in the Alps, you wouldn't make it to the first Saint Bernard."

Irving didn't hear this, he had disappeared into the bedroom, and I could hear him desperately trying to raise the radiophone operator. A futile task at that time of day on our fifteen-party line. I had explained with much patience *before* that we could never get the operator until after five o'clock, when every lumberman, miner and everybody else who worked back in the bush had quit for the day. We were the farthest out in the forest, and our phone signal was much weaker than those who lived or worked nearer Bell Canada's transmitter, so our signal was slower, electronically, so we had to wait until all traffic had ceased before we could communicate. Even if Irving had remembered, he still would have tried to call Peter Fonda—or the Virgin Mary, if he thought he could get her a part in a picture—with Charlton Heston.

"You sure have a lot of nutty friends," Charlie Burke said, sipping the cup of coffee Reiko had provided him.

"Charlie," I said, "I'm thinking of leaving Lost Lake and going back to Hollywood."

Charlie was silent for a moment, then: "During the war I had a picture of Betty Grable pinned up in my flight locker at Hedgerow. She was in a bathing suit, with her hands on her hips, sticking her ass out toward the camera."

"Yeah," I said, "she musta sent out five or six million copies of that picture."

Charlie was shocked. "You're kidding," he said. "It was autographed to me, personally."

"She's fifty-six years old now," I said.

"It was an awful cute ass," Charlie said, a tear in his throat.

"It's still cute," I said. "We did a television show with her not too long ago."

"Some things don't change, do they?" Charlie said, with a sigh of relief.

"Well, Betty Grable's ass didn't," I said.

"Hallelujah," Charlie said. I had made his day.

Irving dashed out of the bedroom, his three remaining strands of hair tousled. He was angry and frustrated.

"That goddamn phone!" he said. "The operator is French!"

"That's not the operator," Reiko said. "That's Mr. Desormeaux—he's a French-Canadian—he uses the phone all the time. He has a lumber camp."

"Well, the son of a bitch never stops talking," Irving said. "I'm trying to get Peter Fonda, and that frog bastard is holding up a ten-million-dollar production with a two-bit lumber mill."

"Why don't you go up and have a little talk with him?" I said sweetly. "I'm sure when he understands the motion picture business, he'll ease up a little on the phone. Then you'll be able to call Peter Fonda or anybody else in Hollywood."

"Let's call Betty Grable," Charlie said.

"Why?" Irving said.

"You never can tell," Charlie said. "She might remember me from the stage door canteen in London. I almost danced with her—on New Year's Eve—during an air raid."

"What the hell is this nut talking about?" Irving said. "I'm try'na close a fifteen-million-dollar deal and he's—"

"Just for that," Charlie said, "you can *walk* back to Chinookville—you're not riding in *my* plane." Charlie started for the door, and the wolf growled at Irving.

"What did I say?" Irving said. "Look, Mr. Burke, if I've done anything to offend—"

"Apologize," Charlie said, his lip curling like Jackie Cooper's used to when he was young and gay and pouty. The wolf growled again at Irving and showed an unnecessary length, I thought, of fang.

"I'm sorry," Irving screamed at the wolf.

"To me," Charlie said.

"Why?" Irving said. "*He's* the one who's gonna bite me."

"Wolves don't bite people," Bobby said. "They bite moose."

"Yeah," Irving said, "but how do we know he isn't having a nervous breakdown and everybody looks like a moose?"

"I think *you're* having a nervous breakdown," Charlie said. "And everybody looks like a wolf."

"Wait a minute," I said. "Irving, why did you come up here? Not that you're not welcome anytime, but tell me what you want and get back to Chasen's."

I knew why he'd come all the way up to Lost Lake. Despite his apparent inability ever to get me a writing job, he did love me and wanted to help. It was just that he was always getting tied up in "big deals" that sidetracked him from his regular nonworking clients. And right now, I felt that he wanted me to take this Hollywood job with Johnny Blackwell, but if I left it up to him, I knew he would never broach the subject, so I said, "Why do you want me to write the Johnny Blackwell movie?"

Irving hesitated, but only for the split second it took for his hair-trigger mind to change gears. "Because it's money. You can't sit up here in this goddamn wilderness for the rest of your life and stare out at that goddamn lake and those goddamn trees and that goddamn blue sky!"

"Why not?" I said, nettled at his insensitivity of the vast and lovely all-enveloping beauty of the Canadian northland.

"Because it just isn't being done."

"We've been here for two years," I said.

"Okay! Okay!" he said. "You proved you could do it. Now forget it and come back."

"We weren't trying to *prove* anything," Reiko said, with some heat. "This is our home and we love it."

I didn't know Reiko felt quite like that, although she always seemed contented enough, but I also knew that didn't mean too much with an Oriental. They have something they call patience. They'll put up with anything because they feel that "this too will pass," but of course in Asia this never happens. They're patient to the point of stupidity. They *accept* rather than try to *change*. I'm speaking of the great masses—not the leaders. The leaders are conniving, contriving, and devious. Their idea of an earthly paradise would be a world of abject slaves with themselves as absolute rulers. This goes for every Asian country without exception. The people are lovely and gentle and compassionate. Their leaders are all Genghis Khans—represented by the William Morris office.

Reiko's defense of what she thought was a deprecation of our northland home was strong indeed. I could see that she was very proud of everything we had and had done in a very remote corner of the world. But even as she bristled at Irving's blooper, I knew, deep in my heart, that she would like to see Disneyland, too.

"You can always come back," Irving said. "Nothing's gonna change around here."

Before I could answer, Irving whipped an envelope out of his inside pocket and said, "Here are your plane tickets," he said. "And I've got you reservations at the Imperial Century Palace."

"What the hell's that?"

"It's new since you were out there," Irving said. "It's the last word in luxury hotel apartments—they built it on the old United Stars film lot. It covers five acres. The rest is oil wells."

"That must be nice," I said, "a luxury apartment building right next to a bunch of stinking oil wells."

"Oh, they don't stink," Irving said. "The management took care of that."

"How?" I said.

"The management gives every apartment owner a percentage of the oil."

"Oh," I said, "that *would* eliminate the stink, wouldn't it?"

"You'd be surprised," he said.

"No, I wouldn't," I said. "I once owned an oil lease on my property in the San Fernando Valley. I got ten dollars per acre per month—"

"Did they ever hit any oil?" Irving asked.

"No," I said. "Just Vaseline." Irving looked puzzled, then his squirrel monkey face let itself go into a sort of tentative grin. "Oh," he said, "that's a joke, isn't it?"

"More or less," I said. The sun was setting over Lost Lake and the amazing golds were changing into fantastic purples with long shafts of pink. The tallest pines were black along the shoreline and the loons were calling to each other across the mirrored water. I forgot about Irving and Hollywood and the money and just sat, enthralled once again by this wondrous extravaganza of light and sound, lost in the warm glow of a simplified world. A world without anything but beauty, peace, and a quiet, incomprehensible sense of being.

My euphoric trance was broken by Reiko. "Jack-san, the generator must be broken again—we have no lights."

A new generator cost about $2,000, plus transportation to Lost Lake, which would be another thousand. And that, Dear Friends of Film Fun, is why I decided to return to Hollywood.

2

AS the day neared when we were to take off for California I grew more and more irritable, apprehensive, and nervous.

Somebody—I think it was Thomas Wolfe, or maybe it was Yvonne De Carlo—once said you can't go back. Anyway, it bothered me. I had tried going back to a few places I had known and loved in my lifetime. Tahiti, Acapulco, Honolulu, Rome, Paris, Cairo, Alaska, San Francisco, and Old New Litchridge in Connecticut, and it was always disappointing—they weren't the same.

Tahiti now has high-rise hotels and 6,000 French troops. The 6,000 French troops are not there to protect the high-rise hotels—or Tahiti. They are there to help France develop its own hydrogen bomb. Why they have to build their own is beyond all comprehension. Why don't they just order one from F.A.O. Schwarz like other countries do?

Acapulco has become the winter Mecca of the jet set. And the jet set now includes everybody with a credit card, which includes everybody. Consequently, the once picturesque and lovely and lonely beaches of that Mexican resort are now covered with solid and not-so-solid flesh, and every day from 9 A.M. to 4 P.M. 736,000 belly buttons are aimed directly at the sun. If everybody coughed at exactly the same moment, there'd be an eclipse.

Honolulu has changed little since I first visited there. It's still overcrowded, dirty and expensive. There *is* one difference: The leis the lovely wahines hang around your neck as you get off your 747 are now made with poison ivy. This gives you an idea of what to expect on your all-expense tour. An "all-expense" tour! It couldn't have been better named.

One airline has an ingenious little ploy to lure tourists to these Pacific islands. They give you (with every air ticket purchased) a coupon book which entitles you to "$200 worth of Hawaii free"—discounts in places of interest, plus seventy restaurants and shops. This intrigued me (not that I ever entertained the notion of taking them up on their kind offer) until I figured out that you could fly into a volcano, take an auto ride, buy a gift, visit a ship, go deep-sea fishing, have your hair washed and set, eat a Royal Hawaiian feast, watch some grass-thatched asses revolve, and buy a shapeless Hawaiian coverall—all on four different Hawaiian islands—and still have $185.10 left in your jolly little discount book. A friend of mine, Mike Belshaw, who is also a professor of economics, says you'd have to stretch your two-week vacation in Hawaii to at least three years to take full advantage of your $200 worth of Hawaii free! Also you'd have to spend away about $2,000 to do it, before taking the big bird back to the mainland and the cobbler's bench.

Rome is still full of lovable Italians, and the Italians must be the most gentle and kind and civilized of all us naked apes, but Rome at the same time is just one strike after another. The garbage men strike, the postal workers strike, the hotel chambermaids strike, the phone company workers strike, the bakers strike, the tourist guides strike, the taxicab drivers strike, and last year the homosexuals struck. I don't know what *they* wanted. Shorter hours?

London is not my old London of The Cheshire Cheese, the Old Curiosity Shoppe, and The Reading Gaol. It's now the London of the crotch-high mini, the art class luncheon, with dirty-footed nudes posing in classic porno tableaux for the ribbon clerks of Berkeley Square, and shiny tin and cellophane office buildings looking directly down on Queen Elizabeth's mint garden.

Paris isn't the same without Alice B. Toklas.

Cairo has lost its warmth without Farouk.

San Francisco's fogs are colder and more penetrating,

and its cable cars are loaded with people who don't use Dial. They use muskrat lure.

Alaska, purchased from Russia for $7,000,000, has been resold to Standard Oil of New Jersey for $1 billion—furnished.

Old New Litchridge, Connecticut, has changed, too. Large areas of lovely woodland have been bulldozed down to make room for the Old New Litchridge open space program. The dear sweet old lady who used to live next door to us when we resided there has gone back to Transylvania, where once every year she dresses in black and journeys to Bela Lugosi's tomb with a tiny bouquet of dead pink mice to lay on his casket, with a card reading, "Bela, baby—why *you?*"

Thomas Wolfe, or was it Yvonne De Carlo, was right. You can't go back, but without a new generator we had no electricity at Lost Lake, and without electricity we had no lights, no telephone and no television, and without television we had no way of knowing whether we were happy. So I quieted my nerves, quashed my irritation, throttled my apprehension, ordered a new generator, and started packing.

3

ON the last day of October we left Lost Lake. The lake water was still, and golden mists were swirling from its surface as the first rays of the sun warmed it. I walked out to the dock where Charlie Burke would soon be arriving in his float plane to take us to Chinookville and Air Canada and California. I watched a long wedge of Canada geese disappearing over the still-dark tops of the towering pines and firs along the shores of the lake, standing like black-clad mourners around an open grave. It looked an early winter with lots of snow, but I wouldn't be there to see it and revel in it. I would be in the land of perpetual sunshine and eternal youth and everlasting enthusiasm. I could withstand perpetual sunshine because I was getting paid enough. Eternal youth I could avoid by not taking my Peter Pan pills and staying away from Sunset Strip, but I wasn't sure I could work up any degree of tolerance toward enthusiasm.

"Got a great idea for a book," a California enthusiast once shouted at me, in the strictest confidence, one steamy day while I was trying to nap on my foam mattress next to my Olympic-size swimming pool in the backyard of my palatial Northridge estate. I was getting unemployment insurance at the time, so I listened to him.

"My great-grandmother was the first white woman in North Dakota," he said. "How's *that* for a story?"

"Great," I said enthusiastically. "Was she captured by the Indians or something like that?"

"No," he said. "You don't seem to get it. My great-grandmother was the *first white woman in North Da-*

kota—it's a *great* story—and *you* can write it—and all I want is a percentage—"

"That's all?" I said. "How much of a percentage?"

"Whatever's fair," he said. "Fifty percent."

"That's fair enough," I said, "for a great story like that. You don't want me to give you a down payment or anything like that, do you?"

"Of course not," he said. "I trust you—just sign here." The Enthusiast shoved an inch-thick contract, covered with blue ribbons, sealing waxes and official-looking stamps all over it, into my hands.

"Go ahead, sign," he said.

"I got this slight touch of arthritis," I said. "I'm going to see my lawyer this afternoon—he's got some pills and—"

"Give it back," the Enthusiast said, grabbing the heavy contract from me and pushing it back into his bulging attaché case. "I don't think you're right for my great-grandmother's story."

This is not an imaginary scene. This has happened to me many times. Somebody always has a relative's life story or their own life story which would make a marvelous book. And they're willing to cut *you* in on your own royalties.

There are many other kinds of enthusiasts in show business—everything—every project or scheme is going to make everybody rich. "It just can't miss!" But unfortunately they do miss. For every hit there must be a million misses. Maybe more. But for every miss, the Enthusiast is ready with another enterprise from his bottomless bag of unworkable enthusiasms.

As I stood there on the motionless dock in the still, cold air of the Canadian sunrise, I wondered if after two tranquil, almost dreamlike years of the deep and peaceful insularity of forest living, I could weather a year in another kind of isolation.

As I turned to go back up the slight rise to the house, I heard a plane. I thought, this of all times, Charlie Burke is early! He wasn't due for another hour, and the thought of leaving an hour too soon angered me. I didn't want to leave at all.

The plane wasn't Charlie Burke's. It was the Ontario Bureau of Mines plane, with its two indefatigable geologists, Handsome Harry, who looked more like Clint Eastwood than a geologist, and Professor Swayne, who looked and acted like Wally Cox.

These two had been poking around Lost Lake and many other lakes in the region ever since we bought the place some five years before, and at first we were very concerned they would discover a mother lode of some precious metal and start another gold rush, or uranium or copper or nickel rush. Especially since Queen Elizabeth, not us, owned all mineral rights; we were more or less smack in the middle of 4,000 square miles of Crown land.

"Back again?" I said, for openers.

"Yeah," Professor Swayne said, with an attempt at a smile which didn't quite make it. Handsome Harry never said anything—he just grinned and grinned and grinned.

"Like I told you before," I said, not quite neighborly, "you start digging and you'll never leave here alive."

"I know," Professor Swayne said. "Mind if we camp over in the cove for a couple of days?"

"It's not my cove," I said. "The queen just lets me use it."

"I hope you haven't disturbed anything," the professor said.

"How the hell do you disturb a cove?" I said.

"Interesting question, Mr. Douglas. Now if you'll excuse us, we have work to do," the professor said.

Handsome Harry stretched his grin to the breaking point and they started to unload their probing gear from the plane.

"Look," I said, feeling a bit sorry for the two with their seemingly endless and hopeless job, "why don't you use one of our cabins—you'll be a helluva lot more comfortable than in a lousy tent."

"Thank you very much, Mr. Douglas," Professor Swayne said between pursed lips, "but it won't make any difference—we're still going to look for mineral deposits."

"Be my guest," I said, with a lavish gesture of hospitality. "Just see that you leave that cove—as you found it. If I discover one little pebble out of place, I'm going to wire Trudeau."

"Who's Trudeau?" the professor asked Handsome Harry. Handsome Harry didn't relax his grin, but the corners of his mouth were beginning to trickle tiny rivulets of tight blood.

When Charlie Burke's Cessna 180 splashed down at the north end of Lost Lake and taxied up to our plane dock, I wanted to tell him it was all a mistake and to go back to the base, but then I thought of that $2,000 generator and a few other expensive little things that I wanted to do to improve our lot, and I immediately started loading the plane with our things, which included some very heavy movie camera cases and equipment.

"You gonna make a movie in Hollywood?" Charlie Burke wanted to know.

"I may make a remake of *The Birth of a Nation*," I said, not too happy with Charlie's question. "And don't worry about the weight; we'll be able to get off the lake all right."

"I'm not too sure about that," Charlie said. "There's no wind and you got an awful lot of stuff here. Why don't you leave some of it behind? It'll be safe."

"Oh, really," I said. "What happened to my aluminum canoe, my six pairs of snowshoes and my fifty dollars worth of canned goods that one day we were away from camp last winter?"

"It's those goddamn snowmobiles," Charlie said. "They can go anywhere."

"Yeah," I said. "But who could wear six pairs of snowshoes?"

"Well, offhand," Charlie said, "I'd say either the June Taylor dancers, or some guy with twelve legs."

"It wasn't the June Taylor dancers—they're too busy wandering around Florida looking for new jobs."

"Then it must be the guy with the twelve legs," Charlie said. "I'll keep my eye out for him." Charlie's face had been eroded down to bedrock by the elements and many years of dealing with the brave hunters who came north each year to stain the virgin whiteness of the new snow with the life blood of a mortally wounded, defenseless animal. *Field and Stream* called them sportsmen. Charlie Burke is more realistic and less given to euphemisms. He calls them faggots with field artillery. Charlie really believes they're latent homosexuals annually trying to reestablish their manhood. I'm inclined to agree. As the Indians say, "Big gun—little prick." But no matter what, Charlie's face never gave him away. To the "sportsmen" he was a great bush pilot who was on their side. He *was* a great bush pilot, but I had the feeling that someday he would ferry a large party of these fearless moose murderers to a remote wilderness lake, wish them luck, then take off and forget them completely until sometime in the spring. If the Ontario Provincial Police should ask him some embarrassing questions, he could always say he went back to pick them up, but apparently they had been mistaken as to which lake they were to rendezvous. There are thousands upon thousands of lakes in northern Ontario, and it would have been easy for the hunting party to pick the wrong lake and easier still for Charlie Burke to get the sun in his eyes and miss their 50-foot SOS stamped out in the snow. This wouldn't stop the animal slaughter, but it would give the local ravens a change of diet.

I think Reiko had some misgivings, too, about leaving our forest home as we jammed ourselves inside the Cessna and Charlie shoved it away from the dock and started the motor. Reiko would never say she was sad, but the tears would come to her beautiful eyes, and her lower lip would slightly tremble.

"Well," I said, like a cheerful undertaker. "This time next year we'll have a brand-new generator."

"I'd rather have a horse," Bobby said. Reiko said nothing, Timothy just gurgled and threw up a little, and I said, "What would you do with a horse up here in the woods?"

"Ride him," Bobby said quite logically.

"You'd get lost in five minutes," I said, also quite logically. "If a horse ever took off with you into the woods and you got off the trail, you'd get lost and maybe we'd never find you. Did you ever think about that?"

"Gee," Bobby answered. "I can't wait till we get to Disneyland."

As the little Cessna gained speed and altitude I turned around for one last look at our now-rapidly shrinking main island and its lovely log lodge. It looked forlorn and lonely and I wondered if we'd ever see it again. At that moment I had some doubt. How could we ever tear away from the neon and frozen orange juice of twenty-first-century southern California and snowshoe back into the nineteenth century of our wilderness home?

The 747 which flew us to the California gold country was crowded. Looking over the other 346 passengers, I wondered about hijackers and if there were any aboard. I hadn't seen Havana since I raced a 4.9 Ferrari through its rain-slick streets way back when. This was the year Juan Manuel Fangio, who was the world's champion, had been kidnapped by Fidel Castro's hillbillies—not for ransom, but so he couldn't participate in the Havana Grand Prix (or whatever it was called). Fidel figured this would spoil everybody's fun, and in a way it did. They don't have the Havana Grand Prix anymore. They don't have any fun things in Havana anymore—except the *David Susskind Show* with Fidel Castro playing David Susskind. He also plays all of David Susskind's guests. It's a seven-hour show, with no commercials, and if you leave your television set to go to the bathroom, you are immediately classified as an enemy of the state and shot. And there's no silly rule about a blindfold. Also the firing squad has been cut down to one man to save ammunition. But you do get a Polaroid picture (in color) of your execution which is sent to your family.

But all this idle thinking about hijacking soon got lost in the wonderful world of euphoria induced by my sleeping pill, which I immediately swallow upon strapping myself into any airplane anywhere. I'm a fearless flyer, but only with the help of a little seconal.

The 747 is a remarkable aircraft. It cruises at a 40,-

000-foot altitude, and if you want to go higher, they have stairs. They also have three movies and twelve toilets. Which gives you something to do at 40,000 feet. I couldn't help thinking of what would happen if all twelve toilets were flushed at the same time over Kansas City. How would the weather bureau report *that?*

My cowardly habit of taking sleeping pills while flying got me into a bit of an embarrassment one night when I was flying into Kennedy Airport in New York, on a quick trip from Toronto. My captain spoke to me over the loud-speaker; he announced that there would be a slight delay of about a half hour in landing and we would circle the airport during that time. This word unnerved me because I had timed my sleep potion to wear off just as we glided onto the Kennedy runway, so I immediately swallowed another pill. I never eat anything in flight or before leaving the ground, so the pill took rather immediate effect. Just seconds after feeling like Lucky Lindy again, my captain announced that we would be landing in three minutes. When the plane doors opened, I tried the sixteen steps down from the airplane and missed every one of them. I was assisted to my feet by three hostesses and an unidentified man, who seemed to be equipped with a cargo hook. These four good Samaritans dragged me through the extremely well-lighted (I thought) waiting rooms (all of them). My legs which were now Jell-o flopped in all directions. At first I tried to explain to anyone within earshot that I was Gene Kelly practicing. Then realizing that this explanation wasn't doing too well, I started screaming to anyone who would listen that I wasn't drunk! No matter how it looked, I *wasn't drunk!* The hostesses and the man with the cargo hook got me into a taxicab and told the driver to take me wherever I wanted to go.

I'll never forget that taxicab driver. As soon as we were out of the airport proper, he asked to see my wallet, for identification purposes. After he had identified me, he handed the wallet back to me and said, "I left you a buck in case you wanna get some coffee." Then he drove me back to the Air Canada building where a skycap took my luggage and the next thing I knew I was on a plane on my way back to Toronto. This time when I heard a voice on the loudspeaker say, "This is your captain speaking . . . ," I didn't listen.

There was a bit of mild excitement when our 747 reached the Los Angeles International Airport and taxied toward the terminal. A little old lady, wearing a Queen Mary hat and a paisley shawl and maxi-bloomers, suddenly pulled out a vicious-looking Luger and ordered the plane to be flown to Forest Lawn. She also demanded to see the pilot. The hostess calmly opened the door to one of the 747's twelve toilets and ushered her inside. A U.S. Army first lieutenant who had been sitting on the stainless steel bowl screamed—the little old lady dropped her Luger which was picked up by a small boy who had spent the entire trip playing Greyhound bus in the aisles, and the little old lady was gently pushed back into her seat, strapped down and given a copy of *Newsweek*.

"She does that every trip," the hostess confidentially explained to me.

"What about the gun?" I said. "She's liable to hurt someone."

"It's a water pistol," the hostess said. "She used to fill it with chicken soup. Then we had a *real* problem. Cleaning bills, you know."

This incident, I felt, set the whole tone of our trip to Hollywood. It really wasn't happening. There was no such place as Oz. But there was.

Irving Laveeeene, my agent, met us at the baggage roulette wheel.

"You're not gonna like it out here," were his first words.

"I know," I said.

"Where's the sunshine?" Reiko said.

"Where's Disneyland?" Bobby said.

Timothy dropped his little plastic bag which had been filled with water and tiny lake trout, which was his favorite toy of the moment. Jesus Christ! All the way from Canada he didn't spill a drop and now in the middle of the Los Angeles airport—!

"What are those?" Irving wanted to know, paling a little.

"Germs from outer space," Bobby said.

"Oh," Irving said, reassured. "The smog will take care of *them!*"

4

IN all the years I put in, in the fun factories of Hollywood, we used to joke (childishly, when we wanted an easy laugh) about the Los Angeles smog. But the joke had grown into a monstrous reality. The sun was shining as though from behind a giant opaque scrim. The people in the waiting room had a strange look about them. They were all deeply tanned but with an overlay of green and gray. "Mommy!" Bobby said. "Mommy, look at the zombies!"

"Shhhhh!" Reiko shhhed. "They can hear."

"Well," Irving said, "I've got my car outside—let's get over to the Imperial Century Palace."

"What's that?" Reiko asked.

"Only the most beautiful apartment hotel in the world," Irving said. "Makes Rockefeller Center look like a Shell station. Ha-ha-ha!"

"We gotta rent a Hertz pickup truck," I said.

"You got that much baggage?"

"No—for the animals."

"Holy Jesus!" Irving said. "You didn't bring that whole zoo with you, did you?"

"Of course not," I said. "Just the two dogs, one wolf and Pussycat."

"Pussycat?" Irving said.

"Pussycat's a mountain lion," Bobby said.

"Pussycat's a mountain lion," Irving repeated dutifully, like a faithful computer memorizing.

"She's a female," Bobby said, "and she's got the hots."

"Heat," I said.

"A female mountain lion and she's in heat?" Irving said,

his eyes starting to glaze over. "I'd better explain this to the Imperial Century Palace—or better still, I'd better stay here at the airport and take a plane."

"To where?" I said.

"Anywhere," he said, "anywhere."

Needless to say, we were not welcomed with open arms at the Imperial Century Palace. We were greeted at the door by the California National Guard, and Efrem Zimbalist, Jr., who flashed his FBI credit card and told us that the Imperial Century Palace had changed its policy and was now an institution for old Tarzans. This didn't sound quite plausible but it did make us feel that we were persona non grata. We settled for a motel about 40 miles from Hollywood, which had been bypassed by *all* the new freeways and would have been glad to accommodate a tribe of pygmies with no baggage. The manager, who was at least eighty, said he *enjoyed* having wolves and cougars and even sometimes people around. He said this even after the first night when Tanuki, the wolf, had howled and Pussycat, the mountain lion had screamed most of the time. We were the only patrons of this off-the-track tourist camp, or we would surely have found ourselves in trouble with the authorities.

House hunting, which I thought would have been attended to by the studio to which Johnny Blackwell was under contract, had somehow been overlooked, so it was up to us. I left Reiko with two savage children and four impossible animals and started out. It was not only very discouraging—it was infuriating. No one who had a house to rent wanted children (I never mentioned the animals).

"What's the matter with children?" I asked one imperious blue-rinsed bitch.

"Children are destructive. Why, if I were to rent my lovely home to someone with children, what would happen to all my lovely antiques?"

"*My* children love antiques," I said. "Every Christmas, they don't want Hot Wheels or Johnny Lightning, or any of those rough toys. They want antiques—maybe a little

china dog that was once owned by Dolley Madison or a
Benedict Arnold snuffbox—you know—things like that."

"You see that tall glass whatnot case in the corner?" she
said. "It's just crammed full of the most precious antique
doll's house furnishings you've ever seen—my great-great-
grandmother brought them to California on a sailing
ship—around the horn."

"That's very interesting," I said, forcing myself to become interested. "Did you ever read *Two Years Before
the Mast* by Richard Henry Dana? It tells all about *his*
trip to California about the same time, and—"

"The last thing I read," the blue-rinsed cobra said, "was
The Deerslayer by James Fenimore Cooper—he's a neighbor of mine. He lives right up the street."

"James Fenimore Cooper! I thought he was dead," I
said.

"That's what they'd like you to think," she said.

"What about F. Scott Fitzgerald?"

"You mean Jimmy's roommate?"

On this note I left. I don't mind a house full of antiques, if we had been lucky enough to rent it, but this
menopausic beldam would have been too much every
month when she showed up on her broom to collect the
rent. Besides, by this time I was so frazzled I couldn't go
back to the motel and face Reiko, so I spent most of that
evening in a small intimate bar, thinking my small intimate thoughts, and trying to remember who Sheilah
Graham used to pal around with—F. Scott or Jimmy. All
I could remember was that she wrote a book, *Too Much,
Too Soon.*

Three weeks later I was still looking for a place to live.
I had put off meeting Johnny Blackwell, which made him
livid, Irving told me, but I had to get my family settled
before I could even conisder writing anything funny for
this marvelous ad-libber to say. And not only that, the
motel owner who had been so friendly at first was showing
signs of incipient rabies, brought on purely by a mental
condition brought on purely by long nights of continuous
wolf howls and puma screeching. This will do it.

We had to have a house with a large enough backyard

area to build a few animal pens. I did find an ideal place up one of the canyons, but two days later after I had signed a lease, the annual California brush fire season started and poof! Feldman Hills was just a charred memory and many twisted Volkswagen lumps.

One lovely spinster, who said she *adored* animals, said she'd be delighted to rent her house to us if we didn't mind her occupying the guest room and doing her cooking in our kitchen. She said she would even help us with our cooking. We were so desperate we almost accepted this idea until I asked around the neighborhood what kind of a woman she was. My first stop was at the house next door, and they told me more than I wanted to hear about this lovely lady: Years ago she had been accused of carefully cutting up two of her female roommates and packaging and labeling them and neatly stacking them in her deepfreeze. She had been put away in an institution for a few years, but after the authorities decided she was harmless because she had had a long time to think it over, she was released.

I went back and asked this too-willing lady, "Have you still got your deepfreeze?"

"Yes," she said, "it's out in the garage—would you like to see it? Just sign here." She handed me a completed lease form. All it needed was my signature.

"I couldn't sign anything without my agent," I said.

"That's quite all right," she said. "You bring him around—as soon as you can." I could picture Irving and me in that deepfreeze. Then I could picture Irving *alone* in that deepfreeze—for the first time *really* representing me.

Finally, in my last desperate hours of sanity, sitting on the edge of our midget-size Hollywood bed, I put in a phone call to the Hollywood Chamber of Commerce and by some strange miracle I got a man who used to work for the Automobile Club of Southern California, an insurance group which passed itself off as a club, and one of my early day feuds. Of course, the man remembered me (how could he forget someone who fought like a tiger over a three-dollar mistake in billing?).

"Well, this is a surprise," I said, surprised.

"Yeah," Charlton Rogers said, "I thought you had been barred from this section of the world for good. Ha-ha-ha." Mr. Rogers had picked up a thin sheen of hick humor since he'd left the auto club and joined the Chamber of Commerce, something he wouldn't have dared cultivate at his former job.

"Look, Mr. Rogers," said, "I'm desperate!"

"But you said you'd only arrived in Hollywood a couple of weeks ago," Mr. Rogers said.

"I didn't mean for money or a girl—or even a fix," I said. "I mean for a place to live." I explained the whole thing to him and he promised to call back within the hour. I didn't know whether I could hold out that long. The wolf howled louder than ever and at the slightest noise. He just used to howl at jet planes and police sirens, but now he let go whenever he heard an owl, or a cricket, or even a toilet flush. No matter what, he missed no opportunity to sound lonely and forlorn, which he was—shut up all by himself in a crummy little motel cabin. There was nothing for him left to do after he had torn down the curtains, and ripped the carpets and the bed to shreds. The motel man didn't know this because naturally he didn't provide maid service to a wolf.

Pussycat, the cougar, also had a cabin to herself.

I couldn't understand much of the mountain lion language but from her wild shrieks, it sounded like "Whoever hears me I love you."

The eighty-year-old manager seemed to be getting sprier by the moment, dashed over, and asked us if we could keep "them goddamn varmints quiet!" It seems that some young honeymoon couple, who had been turned down by every motel from San Fernando to Bakersfield because they had no luggage, had just checked into cabin number eight which was right next door to the "cat house," so to speak, and the old man didn't want to lose them. He thought they might be the beginning of a boom. This was impossible because only we and a few mountain goats knew of this place, but I didn't disillusion the old man. It might be his last chance at immortality, in the manner of Frank Case, of the Algonquin, or maybe Sherman Billingsley, or Toots Shor.

I promised the old man I would do what I could to regain the peace and quiet so necessary to a couple of young humping honeymooners. At the same time I was hoping that *their* screams wouldn't upset Pussycat.

Mr. Rogers called back almost on the button at one hour and told me to be at a certain address in the Roxbury Hills area of West Los Angeles at 8:00 A.M. I was there at 5:30 A.M. So were the cops. By the time I got the whole thing explained to them, it was time to keep my 8:00 appointment.

5

THE Roxbury Hills section of West Los Angeles was where you lived if you were halfway between being somebody and nobody. The houses were all in the price range which could be afforded by the almost affluent—for a few years at least, then the next hopeful would take over and live like a semi-movie star until the pendulum swung the other way and another cycle would begin and end.

Our immediate neighbor was a Sunset Boulevard type of ex-movie queen, who drove a huge vintage Rolls-Royce, which must have been made before Rolls and Royce agreed on what they were manufacturing—automobiles or houseboats. The back seat was larger than most development living rooms. I asked Miss Sunset, which isn't her name, if it had a bar, and she said no, because she was a fanatic teetotaler, but the car did have a soda fountain, complete with stools and a large Moxie sign. This vehicle, which can only be described as Frankensteinian, was hourly waxed by Miss Sunset's butler, who can only be described as Frankensteinian—with a dash of Machiavelli, and a soupçon of Rex Reed. The butler, Quincy, liked me. Because, I suppose, I was the only one who listened to him.

"You know what kinda wax I'm using on this lovely car?" Quincy said one day.

"No," I said. "What kind of wax are you using on that lovely car?"

"Frog wax," he said. "It comes from frogs. Female frogs."

"Why female frogs?" I said.

44

Quincy looked at me almost contemptuously. "Who the hell ever heard of wax from a male frog?" he said.

"You mean this frog wax has something to do with a female frog's glands?"

"What are you—from another world???? Frog wax in a frog is like mother's milk in a mother." Then he turned his full attention to the mechanical monster he was shining to the point of igniting with its own brilliance. I could see that he had derived a satisfaction approaching orgasm the higher the gloss.

"I use mother's milk on my car," I said. "It brings out the bumpers." I didn't wait for Quincy's comment because Miss Sunset was making her grand entrance from the Spanish balcony of her Old English manor house, down the stairs to the cool of her Rumanian courtyard which adjoined her French Provincial patio with its Early American swimming pool. Actually, the swimming pool was early Hollywood which meant it dwarfed today's 20-by-40 footers. Miss Sunset's pool was a few acres smaller than the Pacific and was shaped like her left breast in its heyday. The pool, she confided some time later, had been a disappointment. She had wanted it to be in the form of *both* of her once-splendid equipage, but, alas, her business manager would not allow it. He said any such move would make her liable to taxes in the adjoining county as well. Of course, when I met Miss Sunset, what had once been twin and steaming volcanoes were now mostly an eroded lava flow held in reasonable check by a Cross-Your-Navel bra.

Miss Sunset still acted as if she were the reigning queen of the movies. Her gait as she dipped step by step down the spiral staircase had apparently been choreographed by Busby Berkeley as he imagined Nefertiti would have descended from her bridal bed in the heat of a moonless Egyptian midnight to the waiting arms of her favorite slave. Each foot was precisely placed in front of the other. The toe pointed exactly at a 67½-degree angle. No more, no less. A loose grape carelessly dropped by some long-departed Caesar caused a slight skid from which Miss Sunset gave not the slightest hint of approbation. She maintained her "grace under pressure" to the full. As she descended one could almost hear "Pomp and Circumstance" being played by all the music in the world. As she reached the bottom step she smiled a Mona Lisa smile and let go with a full, resonant and rumbling Walter Matthau belch, rippling the swimming pool with tiny waves. I couldn't help wishing I had had a small portable seismograph; I was curious about the Richter scale reading.

Miss Sunset extended the back of her hand to be kissed, and imagining myself for the moment to be in the Hall of Mirrors in Versailles, I bent over and touched my lips to her soft, Sea and Ski skin. This pleased her. She was glad that she was not living next door to a man who was not hip to the social amenities—a man, who, if not to the manor born, had at least *some* Adolphe Menjou in him. I was happy to pass the acid test because not only was Miss Sunset still a charming woman, with traces of her former exotic beauty remaining, but she knew about all there was to know about Hollywood from Harlow to *Hair*. I asked her if it were true that some girls would go to bed with a Hollywood somebody to get a part in a picture.

"How do you think Fay Wray got that part in *King Kong?*" she said, amused at my naïveté.

"You don't mean—?" I said, crushed at this shocking revelation about the chief cause of my boyhood itch.

"Yep," she said. "Fay told me herself. She said it was the most horrendous night she had ever spent."

"Poor Fay," I said mistily.

"Yes," she said. "Who would have thought that King Kong was insatiable?"

"How about Fay?" I said.

"Good thing she was wearing a diaphragm, I told her," Miss Sunset said.

On thinking it over, what Miss Sunset didn't know about Hollywood she extemporized so well that everything seemed to be the whole truth, which when you come right down to it is a helluva lot more entertaining than the real Hollywood. I lived there for twenty callow years and not once did I get invited to an orgy. And at that age, God knows I needed an orgy, badly. Maybe even two or three. But so much for a misspent youth.

"Did you know," Miss Sunset said, using her peacock feathered lorgnette as a wand for emphasis, "that John Wayne is actually a midget?"

"Oh, come on now, Miss Sunset, I've seen him in so many movies that—"

"You mean those *cowboy* movies?" she said. "You know how they do it? They use short mountains and Duke rides a dachshund."

"Oh, I see," I said, "a joke, huh?"

"One of your own," she said. "I've read some of your books."

I really didn't remember that joke, but I'm glad Miss Sunset did. I made a mental note to put it somewhere in the Johnny Blackwell movie script. Hoping that he understood it, although there wasn't much to understand. The mental machinery of a comic was a very fragile commodity. In the past I've had some of these "funny" fellows question some of the greatest jokes, which I myself have tried out on audiences in nightclubs and television. "What does it mean?" is their favorite question, which churns me up almost to the point of saying, "What the hell do you care what it means if it gets a big laugh?" I never say this because most comedians spend most of their lives on the border of a complete nervous breakdown, and I don't want to be the instrument that pushes them over the edge. Not unless I can be there when it happens with my home movie camera. Which is something else I've often thought of: what a beautiful hobby—a full set of complete nervous breakdowns of all the famous comedians in color and slow motion with Debussy's music.

"Would you care for some tea?" Miss Sunset said. I said I'd love some, and Miss Sunset clapped her hands like some very aristocratic mandarin, and in 15 or 25 minutes Quincy showed up, wiping his female-frog-wax-covered hands on a filthy remnant of cheesecloth.

"What's the problem?" Quincy said.

"We'd like some tea."

"It's against the law," Quincy said and started to head back to the hoary Rolls.

"In a cup!" screamed Miss Sunset demurely.

"Jesus Christ!" Quincy said as he turned in the opposite direction, toward the kitchen. "What won't they think of next!"

Our neighbors on the other side of us in Roxbury Hills were Mr. and Mrs. Bruce Yarrish, the do-gooders. We learned of their avocation the first day we moved in. Before we had had time to get the coffeepot on the stove, Blanche Yarrish was tapping on our door (I think with her nose) and in a thrice she was inside the house telling us how pleased she would be if we contributed maybe a hundred dollars to the Bibles for Biafra Fund.

"But I thought they lost," I said.

"All the more reason they need Bibles." Blanche Yarrish smiled.

"How would it be if I gave two dollars for Bibles and ninety-eight for rifles?" I said.

"I heard you were quite a character," Blanche Yarrish said, still smiling—with some effort, now.

"Not anymore I'm not," I said. "Now I'm an eccentric millionaire who picks people's names out of the phone books and gives them a million dollars—provided they don't tell anybody."

"What about the Internal Revenue Service?" Mrs. Yarrish said, exposing most of her canine teeth, which I'm sure were capped (by a dentist who specialized in beavers).

"That's it," I said. "I'm not only an eccentric millionaire, I'm also a sadist."

Mrs. Yarrish mumbled something about hoping we would be unhappy in our new home and left. I'm not even sure she opened the door.

"She'll be back," Reiko said. Then she added, "I don't like neighbors. Here, I'm not going to make friends with anybody."

"Here we go again," I said. "Two years in the Canadian bush and you complained at least once a week that we didn't have any neighbors, and just as soon as we move back to civilization, you're beefing about them. It was the same thing when we lived in Connecticut. Someday you've got to make up your mind. You either like people or you don't."

"I'm not going to make up my mind," Reiko said.

"There are two things," I told her, "that can drive you crazy—indecision and procrastination." As soon as I said this I knew I was in for an all-day explanation.

"What does—" Reiko said before I cut in on her.

"Forget it," I said. "Some long winter evening—when we're back in Canada—I'll tell you."

"I'm not going back to Canada," Reiko said.

"Why not?"

"No neighbors."

We had other neighbors in Roxbury Hills. There seemed to be no shortage. Unfortunately. In back of us, on our postage stamp acreage, we had the dog lovers, Mr. and Mrs. Burgerbits, we called them. They had seven dogs. All big blue ribbon winners and all mouth so far as we knew. When we looked at the house, when we were house hunting in Roxbury Hills, it was in the daytime, and the unholy seven were asleep. Resting what was left of their vocal chords, I presume. We were totally unaware of the existence of these seven canine superfiends until our first night. Wolf packs in full cry after a faltering moose were nothing compared with the American Kennel Club's glass-shattering canine choir. And somewhere, I suspected, Mr. and Mrs. Burgerbits were sheltering an oversexed bull elk who joined the group on particularly still nights.

Our young wolf and Pussycat, the cougar, along with Doggie, the Pomeranian, and Chibi, the Malamute, were not too thrilled about being forced to live so close to what must have sounded to them like the Hounds of Hell—plus "The King Sisters Celebrate the St. Valentine's Day Massacre" (one of their better specials).

Mr. and Mrs. Burgerbits, on the other hand, were incensed that they were suddenly living next door to a semi-zoo, and promptly complained to the chamber of commerce, the police and the Better Business Bureau, and additionally, a few days later, to the Avon lady, who instantly crossed us off the list as prospective heavy buyers of Tensor's Turtle Oil. Mrs. Burgerbits also blacklisted us with Jehovah's Witnesses—leaving us without any precise date as to when the end of the world was due, forcing us to live from day to day and not subscribe to anything for more than the regular thirteen-issue trial.

Actually, nothing happened. The police were much more concerned with figuring out ways to avoid being killed by the flower children at love-ins than to be bothered by a rabid wolf, a ravening cougar, a bloodthirsty Malamute, and a poison Pomeranian. But they did make a show of coming around in a black and white police car with a screaming siren just to please Mr. and Mrs. Burgerbits, who, it seemed, were old settlers in Roxbury Hills. They had been there before the first mud slide. And the first bulldozer. And the first developer. Or maybe it was all three of these that arrived on the scene at the same time—like the Four Horsemen minus one.

Nightly, from sundown to sunup, the Burgerbits' animals barked—singly, in unison, and in harmony (using the quarter-tone scale with many countermelodies). This was always with the obbligato of the horny elk; this blood-chilling moaning may not have been a horny elk at all—it may well have come from Mr. Burgerbits himself because of his famed (around the neighborhood) indigestion. He had, explained a not-too-kindly neighbor, the same digestive apparatus scientists claim for Vesuvius. This may or may not be true, but apparently whatever he had was hooked up to some amplification system with unblowable tubes. A simple hamburger with onions would set him up for the "1812 Overture." The reports echoing through the hills were much more impressive than the real cannon used in the first performance of this piece back in the old Vienna Opera House.

Finally, after gracelessly enduring a month of this nightly Brobdingnagian tidal wave of sound, I paid a call on Mr. and Mrs. Burgerbits. As they opened the door (they seemed to work as a team) I said, "About your dogs—"

"Oh, yes," Mr. Burgerbits said, "I hope you'll be at the dog show in Pasadena."

"I wouldn't go to Pasadena if they were having a Brontosaurus show," I said.

"That's not until *next* month," Mrs. Burgerbits said, doing her best not to impersonate Billie Burke.

"Your dogs," I said, trying not to be put off, although a Brontosaurus show sounded intriguing. "They bark all night long. Every night!"

"Dogs gotta bark," Mr. Burgerbits said.

"Yes," added Mrs. Burgerbits, "and fish gotta swim and birds gotta fly."

"And I gotta love one gal till I die," Mr. Burgerbits said, grabbing his wife around the waist, waltzing her away somewhere into the dim recesses of their Lysol-scented domicile. I went back to our place. I could see that formal complaints would mean nothing. I had to use other methods.

I had a book on booby trapping, which was put out by Grove press in paperback (so everybody could afford it), but I decided this idea was too dangerous in a neighborhood where children did not know the meaning of the word "fear." They knew the meaning of quite a lot of other four-letter words, but—

I decided to combat the Burgerbits' barking-dog case by another method I had quite successfully used some years before in another California neighborhood. I waited until the Burgerbits' dogs were in particularly good voice and I recorded them on my tape recorder. All ten hours of their continuous barking. Then the next morning, just as the sun was rosy pinking its way over the purple hills, and the dogs, exhausted, had wended their way to their respective doghouses and deep sleep, I started my tape recordings of their previous night's concert. I had had the foresight to buy an ear-slicing electric amplifier and the noise was absolutely catastrophic—to anyone who had not been through the Battle of the Bulge or the Meuse-Argonne campaign.

I gave it some time, expecting the police, the National Guard, and the Burgerbits to come smashing down my front door and demanding what the hell???? But nothing. Nothing happened. Outside, little children played potsy in the middle of the traffic. The postman cheerfully whistled his way up and down the street. The Good Humor man (silenced by the city authorities) sneaked along on Tootsie Roll tires—using hand signals instead of bells on the neighborhood kiddies. But nobody. Nobody! Paid the slightest bit of attention to the absolutely loudest world noise since Krakatoa!

I went over to the Burgerbits' house and knocked on their door, which was immediately opened. I couldn't make myself heard over the sound of my amplifying system of their dogs, but somehow they understood (I thought) and Mrs. Burgerbits ducked out of sight for a moment and came back with two complimentary tickets for the Pasadena dog show. Then they gently closed the door and left me. I went back to our house and shut off the tape recorder and immediately everyone in the street stood stock-still—wondering.

I gave up. I started drinking and smoking again.

Across the street from us lived the Flyer, who was a pilot with some commercial airline. He had a darling Anne Hathaway cottage, which looked like a hangout for queer trolls and was painted purple, which blended nicely with its silver tinsel thatched roof, gingerbread door and opaque candy windows, and surrounded by an entirely plastic rose garden, which only had to be washed—not watered.

"Flying today?" I would say whenever we met.

"Don't be silly," he said. "We got a union." I've known many airline pilots in my life, but I've never known one when he wasn't having a day off. I'm beginning to believe that those thousands of jumbo jets in holding patterns over our airports are being flown by a little old lady with a large push button computer in Balls, Illinois. God help us all if *she* joins a union!

The Flyer, who was a bachelor and looked like a marked-down George Hamilton, took advantage of the fact.

He had girls. He had a clientele like he was the first man on earth. Or the last. All sizes. All shapes. All colors beat a path to his better (I presume) mousetrap. The traffic on Lola Lane (the name of our street) was unbelievable, but not, according to the neighborhood old timers, unusual. When we first moved in, I thought we were living across the street from a world-renowned abortionist who also gave lollipops.

The Flyer, who I'm sure is a reincarnation of Alexander the Great, had a dash of Ronald Coleman in him because he treated each of his moving-belt harem as if she were Mrs. Miniver. No matter how much the path to his house looked like the line-up during Easter Week at Radio City, everyone was given the red carpet treatment. This much I could see from across the street. At certain intervals the front door was flung open and a large group was allowed to pass into what I presumed to be waiting rooms, and always in the background I could hear the strains of "Off we go into the wild blue yonder" while our hero kissed the hand of each and every new arrival. Some giggled and some fainted, but all were admitted with warmly royal gestures.

One day, just for the hell of it, I asked him, "Who are all those girls who come to your house?"

"Friends of Mother's," he said. Then, observing my eyebrows, he explained. "Mother was a Dale Carnegie graduate."

"Oh," I said.

"She was also a hooker," he said.

"Oh," I said again, readily understanding how much farther a girl could go in this profession with the aid of a Dale Carnegie diploma tucked under her bed. Or better still—framed on the wall. Right next to her autographed photos of August von Wassermann, and Doctor Ehrlich and his magic bullet.

After a few months as our neighbor, the Flyer suddenly moved out. It was in all the papers. He flew a 747 jet to Cuba. It wasn't a hijack as everyone at first believed. It was just that he had a 747 buyer in Havana. And I thought he was just another pretty face.

6

DOWN through the long, lovely years, I have written funny words for comedians. Sometimes, because of the faulty diction, or the absolute stubborn resistance of the audience, they didn't come out funny. I always featured a huge sign in my office, IT LEFT HERE FUNNY! This sign used to irritate and infuriate the comic personalities I was writing for. Which, of course, was its sole purpose.

I also had an enormous blowup photo of the moon enclosed in a frame. The rugged surface of the moon was dotted with tiny colored flags. Under this I had a sign: THERE IS AN A&P SUPERMARKET NEAR YOU. All of the comics, except one, either ignored this moon madness or shot furtive glances in its direction—not daring to ask what the hell it meant. Johnny Carson was the only one who ever mentioned it out-loud. His comment was, "I wonder how much a jar of instant coffee cost in the Sea of Tranquility?"

All the comedians I have either written for or am acquainted with seem to be more or less sane, and more or less gentlemen. Not that being a gentleman is essential to success in any business. Quite the reverse, so it seems. Maybe Leo Durocher was right when he said that "nice guys finish last." At least the way it is going for Leo at the moment, he must be a helluva nice guy.

There were some eccentrics among the comical gentry which was to be expected in such a soul-barbecueing business. The very nature of their work and their everyday strict discipline (if they were any good) would tend to make a semi-flippo out of Saint Francis, if he had been a comic instead of a conservationist.

The every waking hour of the comic's day puts a pressure on him that no other profession—or hobby—comes close to. A *comedian* is expected to be *funny!* On- and off-stage. If the gas jockey at the filling station says "good morning" to a Bob Hope or a Jack Paar, a sidesplitting retort is the very least the jock will settle for. If this is not forthcoming, the comedian is marked down as a dullard, or just plain unfriendly. "The son of a bitch thinks he's a big shot just because he makes a million dollars a week" will be part of the multi-told tale. Bob Hope might throw a funny line because he has never stopped telling jokes since he was flattened as a child boxer back in his Cleveland hometown. With Bob it's a marvelously effective defense. Jack Paar, on the other hand, if any strange gasoline attendant had had the audacity to wish *him* a "good morning" would probably react by resolving never to fill up his tank ever again. He might even send a twenty-page note to the president of Texaco demanding an explanation. Jack has always been a great short-note writer, and I have trunks full of Paar's acid missiles, accumulated over a twenty-year period, all of them telling me why he can't *possibly* use the material I have written for him. I'm still writing material for him and he's still telling me why he can't use it and I'm still enthralled by his great personal charm and unlimited integrity.

Red Skelton was and is something else again. I started to write for him when he first came to Hollywood to M-G-M pictures and radio. Red, in those long-ago days, laughed at everything, and he still does, and still remains near the top in the Neilson ratings, which he thinks are pretty funny, too. He once told me in strictest confidence (Red has the inside dope on everything) that the Neilson people's research staff consists solely of two deaf little old ladies with cataracts, living in Nonesuch, Maine, and who don't even have a set. They depend on their arthritis to tip them off whether a TV show is good or not. If they're in pain, it's good. This may or may not be true—it depends on which source you listen to. The shows on top believe in the Neilson system like they believe in God and Ajax. The shows which are faltering say it's the biggest fraud since Billy Graham cured Tiny Tim's nose (he made it into several smaller noses and a very unusual ashtray—engraved "Souvenir of Brighton Beach of 1976," a memento far ahead of its time). The Reverend Mr. Graham's miracle was looked upon with suspicion by a small group of the Oral Roberts Fan Club of Coos (erotica at its most insidious) Bay, Oregon.

However, when I decided to come out of the woods and write again for one of this privileged class, I made a big mistake in my choice of comedian. I picked Johnny Blackwell, which isn't his name or anywhere near it in sound or spelling. He turned out to be a bastard, but he paid well and was reasonably afraid of me, which was a condition I had found, during most of my writing life, very conducive to being able to control, to some degree, the savagery which can be brought on by the vicissitudes of a very exacting and untrustworthy trade. The pursuit of laughter and the agony of not being able to capture it can lead to remarkable cruelties and unspeakable ruthlessness. If it so happened that a comedian's very own dearly beloved mother had been responsible for his losing a laugh, or faltering in his timing, I'm sure the comedian would enjoy disemboweling her on the spot, with an appropriate witticism to cover up what might prove to be an awkward moment in the flow of an otherwise smooth comedic performance. Some funny men would draw and quarter their whole family if they thought it would get a laugh during their first appearance on the *Ed Sullivan Show*. And I'm sure that Ed would thoroughly approve, if he noticed at all, and go on to introduce Liza Minelli in the audience.

My introduction to Johnny Blackwell occurred in Hollywood, or to be more accurate, Bel Air, which is a few miles away out Sunset Boulevard and a few light-years away from Sioux City, which Hollywood has become with the passing of Joseph Von Sternberg.

Johnny Blackwell's home looked like something that should have been perched overlooking the Rhine. It was a castle. Albeit a castle of many styles and moods—from early Rudolph Valentino to late Montreal Habitat 68. From the distance it could have been a Moorish village with some extremely phallic minarets. The closer you got to it, the more it became Bel Air and Beverly Hills.

The castle gates were electric and were embossed with two enormous letters, *J* and *B,* which looked like neon, and I'm sure they were. From a distance the tourists thought it was an ad for scotch whiskey, and maybe it was—I'm sure Johnny Blackwell didn't pay for all that neon.

After announcing myself over the roadside telephone, the gates swung majestically open and I was quite disappointed that King Richard didn't ride through on his way to the Crusades or the Farmer's Market.

I had to gun my car quite strongly to make it up the steep Bel Air hill to a second set of gates which were guarded by a surly watchman, who reluctantly opened them for me to pass into the interior courtyard. I couldn't help thinking that with all these precautions, the Idols of the Silver Screen still get themselves robbed, stabbed, raped and otherwise molested quite regularly. There must be something wrong with the system. Maybe there *is* something to be said for living in Texas. Then again—?

After I had parked my car in the area marked SERFS, I pushed the front doorbell and wasn't disappointed to hear sweet bells playing the comedian's theme song: "It's So Good to Be with You Tonight." A peephole with an eye centered in it told me that I was being inspected. I was about to place my hand against the wall and spread my legs so I could be searched for weapons, but the door opened before I could. The butler, whom I'm sure doubled as a cheap hired killer on his Thursdays off, beckoned me with a head jerk to follow him. I felt as if I were in an old George Raft movie as we proceeded down long hallways to a golden oak door. The butler knocked three times. Nothing happened. He knocked three times again. Nothing happened.

"Maybe you're supposed to say, 'Open sesame,' " I said.

"He's got some broad in there with him," the butler said.

"Princess Grace?" I said.

"Is she a tall brunette with big knockers?" the butler said.

"You're thinking of John Wayne," I said.

The butler knocked again and a muffled "Come in" responded. As we entered, Johnny Blackwell was zipping up and the tall brunette with big knockers was straightening her lips.

"So you're Jack Douglas," Johnny Blackwell said, in a rather challenging tone, I thought.

"Uh-huh," I said, without any emotion one way or the other. The tall brunette with the big knockers and the butler left us alone.

"I usually write all my own stuff," Blackwell said, "but what with my picture commitments and my personal appearances and a lot of other things, I just don't seem to have the time anymore."

"I know," I said. I had heard this line before. Many, many times before. Most comedians always write their own stuff. That's why you always see those long lists of writers' names on the credits at the end of every comedy show.

"Yeah," continued Blackwell. "I know my style better than anybody."

"What happened to Bill Glass and Charlie Weatherspoon?" I said. These were two writers who had written his stuff for the past ten years. "Didn't they work out?"

"No," Blackwell said, "they were getting fat and lazy—besides, they could never really pinpoint my personality. You know, I'm sorta special. In the first place I don't do jokes." That line again, I thought. I had never yet met a comic who would ever admit that he did jokes. The word "jokes" seemed demeaning to them. Small time. Nevertheless, no matter what they called them, they were "jokes." Maugham did jokes and so did Bernard Shaw. Maybe they surrounded them with an aura of legitimacy and literacy, but they were still jokes. "Maybe I won't be able to pinpoint your personality either," I said, "because I write jokes."

"Don't worry about it," Blackwell said. "It's gonna work out fine. How about some lunch?"

"Well—" I hesitated.

"I never eat lunch," Blackwell said in a voice that disapproved of my gluttony. This strengthened a secret resolve in me that from now on I would eat lunch three times a day just to prove to myself that this clown wasn't in charge of the world—yet, anyway.

"I had lunch before I came," I said.

"At ten o'clock in the morning?" he said, lighting a monogrammed L&M.

"I'm still on Canadian time," I said, not wishing to start a fight at our first meeting.

"Oh, yeah," he said, "you just got out of the woods, didn't you? How could you stand it up there?"

"Remarkably well," I said.

"Yeah," he said. "But—no broads—no nothing."

"I'm married," I said.

"What's that got to do with broads?" he said.

"Come to think of it," I said, "I never looked at it that way."

"Wait'll you're in Hollywood a little while," he said, chuckling lasciviously.

"I lived here for twenty-five years."

"And you didn't have broads?"

"I had *all* of them," I said, stretching the truth only slightly.

Johnny Blackwell looked at me with what I thought was new respect. "What have you got in mind for the new season?" he said after a moment and a distinct change of attitude. His eyes narrowed into malevolent slits. Now he looked like the man who asks the questions in a Spanish dungeon.

"I'm a lot older now," I said. "I won't be able to handle as many—I don't think—not on just *plain* Geritol."

"I'm not talking about broads now," Blackwell said. "So stop trying to be funny."

"That's my job," I said.

There was a long ominous silence after this, broken only by the deadly ticking of an asthmatic grandfather clock, which must have been used in every Hitchcock picture that was ever made.

"Why don't you carry a wristwatch like everybody else?" I said, referring to the grandfather clock, which was also a very asthmatic joke. At that moment the door opened, and an accountant-type man entered, but dressed better.

"Hi, Johnny," he said, then to me, "Oh, you must be the new writer."

"Yeah," I said, "Charles Dickens." I stuck out my hand and grabbed the stranger's milky paw. His hand felt like it had had all the bones removed long ago.

"I'm Marty Goodfellow," the stranger said. "I'm Johnny's manager. Johnny Blackwell," he continued, "is probably without a doubt the funniest man alive. He doesn't need writers—"

"He told me," I said, "before you got here."

"What he needs is *assistance*," Marty Goodfellow continued. "Good solid, surefire laugh-getting assistance."

"He needs a good right arm," I said.

"No," Marty said. "No—*I'm* his good right arm!"

"Oh," I said.

"What he needs is somebody he can trust," Marty said.

"How about you?" I said.

"That's not my department," Marty said. "I mean he needs someone he can count on in a pinch."

"Yeah," Johnny said. "That's what I need. Somebody I can talk to. You know—try out my stuff on."

"What about the audience?" I said.

"Oh, shit!" Johnny said. "What the fuck do *they* know?"

"You're right," I said.

"Johnny's always right," Marty said.

"What the fuck do *you* know?" Johnny said to Marty.

"You *see?*" Marty said to me. "Didn't I *tell* you?"

"I think I'll go look around Hollywood," I said. "Maybe I'll stop in at the Stage Door Canteen and dance the lindy with Cornel Wilde." I got up to leave.

"Yeah," Marty said, "that's a good idea. Get acclimated. I'll call you in an hour. Where're you staying?"

"In a trailer in back of the Beverly Hills Hotel," I said.

"Good central location," Marty said. "Call you in half an hour."

"Don't you want the phone number?" I said. "It's Crestview 6-1526."

"Good," Marty said, "I'll call you in fifteen minutes."

I got out of there before I lost my Hollywood tour of inspection altogether.

7

BEFORE starting to work on the new Johnny Blackwell movie, to be called *The Devil and the Hot Virgin*, which I'm sure you won't believe, I had a lot of time on my hands. It seemed they couldn't settle on a story idea and were having trouble with the casting, and also, according to the trade papers, they were having trouble finding a director with enough bravado to tackle this particular project, which didn't come as a surprise because directors were a strange group—the good ones insisted on seeing a script, or at least a semblance of a script before they made up their minds whether they'd like to direct it. We didn't have a script. All we had was a title, which was taken from a book which might have been a big best seller in the Australian outback, but nowhere else, so far as anyone could ascertain.

The Devil and the Hot Virgin in its original book form had 567 racy pages about a Peace Corps worker who had gone into the Amazon jungles to teach the natives how to cook minute rice, and had become involved in local politics which concerned a witch doctor, a virgin and the Devil, who took the form of the omnipresent Mount Goo-boo, an active, irritable and lecherous volcano who demanded a daily sacrifice of one virgin. The story, in the book, concerned the Peace Corps worker's efforts to get the horny volcano to cut it down to one virgin every *other* day and the displeasure this interference from an outsider brought to the old witch doctor, who had had things his own way for some fifty years.

After I had sweated out the reading of this stirring tale,

I called Marty Goodfellow. "What part does Johnny Blackwell play?" I said. "The virgin or the volcano?"

"Jesus Christ!" Marty said. "Here we go with the snotty cracks from the writers!"

"I'm not being snotty," I said. "I'm a beautiful human being. It's virtually impossible for me to be snotty."

"Bullshit!" Marty said cleverly.

"Look me up in the Yellow Pages," I said, "under 'Beautiful human beings.' "

"Johnny is the *Peace Corps worker!*" Marty said. "But all that's been changed."

"To what?" I said.

"Well," Marty said, reluctantly, I thought, "Johnny is now a monk, high up in a hospice, of the Great Saint Bernard Pass, in the Swiss Alps, and he discovers this cute little virgin in the snow—she's struggling against a terrific snowstorm, and she's got a baby in her arms."

"How do you explain the baby if she's a virgin?" I said practically.

"How the hell do I know?" Marty screamed. "That's what we hired writers for!"

"I got an idea," I said quickly. "This monk, high up in a hospice, of the Great Saint Bernard Pass, in the Swiss Alps, forgets his vows when he sees this cute little virgin with the baby."

"Yeah," Marty said, drooling audibly, "and right there in the snow they have an affair."

"Great," I said, "and afterward, or maybe before and during—they drink brandy."

"Where the hell they gettin' the brandy from?" Marty said.

"Marty," I said, "you must be kidding. A man of the world like yourself don't know about those Saint Bernard dogs with the little casks hanging around their necks—"

"You mean," Marty said, "they're carrying brandy?"

"All the time," I said, "all the time."

"I dunno," Marty said, "I dunno. Sounds *weird—dogs* carrying *brandy!*"

"We can update it," I said. "They can carry pot."

"Yeah!" Marty said, as if he had just discovered a cure

for penicillin, "yeah—lemme talk to Johnny about this. I'll get back to you."

This was the way, I presume, this "property" (as scripts are known) had been presented to the various directors who were deemed important enough to handle this precious package. It was promptly turned down by Hy Averback, a great comedy director and the genius who made Peter Sellers funny (at last) in *I Love You, Alice B. Toklas.* Hal Kanter, father of *Julia,* starring the loveliest milk chocolate of all, Diahann Carroll (I wish they had bussed me to *her* school!), put an obituary notice (his) in the *Daily Variety,* so they'd stop pestering him. Gene Saks, who had guided Goldie Hawn up the rocky path to an Academy Award Oscar, although he adored the story, was very busy at the moment growing a new beard, which he said took up most of his day. Jerry Lewis, who was between Johnny Carson subbings, declined because they would not give him complete artistic control.

Speaking of Jerry Lewis, I wish someone would write the life story of this great and compassionate man. If there's any advice a father can give his child today, to which he will listen, it's: "This is America—*forget* Lincoln and the Boy Scouts of America—be like *Jerry Lewis.*"

All during this desperate search for a director and certain actors, I was told to think up ideas to go with the title *The Devil and the Hot Virgin,* and to which I devoted at least fifteen minutes every day. This procedure was typical of Hollywood. They had bought a book, which everyone agreed would make a great movie, but after a while and many story conferences, everyone agreed the book stank and could never make a movie in a million years, then they retained the book title and thought up an entirely different story to go with it. This was what I was supposed to be doing in my ivory tower high up in the Roxbury Hills, where on a clear day you could see air pollution at its most efficient.

I would jot down a few plots stolen from one of my tremendous collection of books on the art of plotting, including one volume in Braille, where dot meets dot, dot loses dot and dot gets dot. These quickly noted notes would satisfy Marty Goodfellow and Johnny Blackwell that I was earning my money, and did nothing to louse up the rest of my day, part of which I devoted to my large collection of feuds:

The Chrysler Corporation is rumored to be the manufacturer of fine automobiles. A rumor undoubtedly started and perpetuated by the Chrysler Corporation.

We had been one of the many trusting souls who had bought a new Chrysler 300 hardtop, with a 50,000 mile or five-year guarantee—whichever came first. What came first was a tremendous explosion which blew the engine apart. This engine, which was apparently designed by the "Mr. Fix-it" editor of *Popular Mechanics* and put together by retarded trade school apprentices, would not start if the weather was too damp, too dry, too hot, too cold, or too perfect.

After the initial explosion, the wrecked engine was replaced. A four-hour job, which took *six weeks,* and we had no more trouble with explosions. Now our main concern was fire. The new engine caught fire three different times, and Reiko, carrying Timothy, escaped being barbecued by a very narrow margin each time.

My letters to Mr. Virgil Boyd, the president of the Chrysler Corporation, were always answered politely and promptly by some public relations man who had no idea he was dealing with Geronimo. Then Mr. Boyd left his lofty post as Mr. Number One, presumably because of his inability to borrow any more money to keep the Chrysler Corporation from going the way of the *Saturday Evening Post.* Now my letters of anguished protest go to Mr. Riccardo, the new president of the Chrysler Corporation. Mr. Riccardo handles things differently. My letters are answered, but the answers are shorter, more sincere and more to the point—they sincerely and most respectfully urge me to go shit in my hat, pull it down over my ears and call myself Mary Pickford. *Their* wording is slightly more euphemistic, but the meaning is very clear.

In the event that anyone thinks I am being unfair in my criticism of the Chrysler Corporation, let me hasten to add that their 50,000-mile or five-year warranty is strictly adhered to—if the ashtrays in your Chrysler wear out within this period, they cheerfully replace them. It may take six or eight weeks and cost you a small $25 or $30 service charge, but to the Chrysler Corporation, living up to their warranty is a sacred duty.

I'm glad there are organizations like the Chrysler Corporation. If nothing else, it restores your faith in cancer.

If I sound bitter, and misanthropic, and cynical, and pessimistic, gloomy, and dismal, and you think I'm about to bite into the cyanide capsule I've concealed under my tongue these many years, you're wrong. It's just that I look at the world we're living in through the eyes of an innocent child, which is very difficult to do because most innocent children's eyes are goddamn hard to see through.

In spite of my horrendous experiences, I'm not an "Up the Establishment" man at all. I'm very much pro-establishment. I *still* believe that the American Telephone & Telegraph Company will someday permit its stockholders to share in *some* of the profits. I still have great faith in the U.S. Postal Service, even though I did get a postcard from Amelia Earhart just last week. I also believe in the little red shoes Judy Garland wore in *The Wizard of Oz* which Elizabeth Taylor paid $15,000 for some time ago at an M-G-M studio auction, only to find that they didn't fit (Richard is now wearing them around the house).

I still believe in vitamin tablets, which cost $1 a thousand to make, and sell for $10 a hundred. I don't get upset about this because I know it's the packaging which boosts the price. Packaging costs money, but it's also convenient. Suppose that Arrid was sold loose and you lived in an especially sweaty area—you'd have to bring your own pail. Those little dab jars are a lot more convenient—albeit more expensive—but it's worth it to safeguard from offending, which we all must do, unless, of course, we are rich with money, then it doesn't matter, no matter what the commercials say—you can smell like last year's ape and still be immensely popular with everybody.

There are so many things which upset so many people. A friend of mine, Allan Schwartz, who is a part-time farmer and a part-time college professor, becomes incensed at this new shaving cream which heats up when applied to the unshaven face.

"How decadent can we get!" Professor Schwartz screams. "My *father* shaved with cold shaving cream. *I* shave with cold shaving cream, and, goddamn it, my *kids* are gonna shave with cold shaving cream! I'll see to *that!*"

Professor Schwartz, I think, has made too quick a judgment about hot shaving cream. It must be a tremendous time-saver and convenience to an undertaker, in his efforts to well groom an untidy stiff who hadn't had the decency to take a quick shave before he passed on.

There are some things (not many) which bug me, but over which I have not yet been able to find the time to get a good feud started. For instance, I thought one morning, as I was staring past my typewriter and its *Devil and the Hot Virgin* story problem to a man on the small hill next to our small hill, who was cutting his lawn with a pair of cuticle scissors, but I wasn't thinking about him—I was thinking about the many things we can, and should, do without in this life. For instance, in our spiritual lives, who needs all those middlemen, with their giant revival meetings, standing between us and God? Why do we have to confess our sins in front of 80,000 people in Yankee Stadium? Why do we have to stand there in the hot sun and tell everybody that we once screwed a chicken? Now, if the *chicken* were standing there in the hot sun describing some of *her* experiences. . . .

If I may be permitted an aberrational aside—a German friend of mine, a veteran of the German army of World War II, fucks pizzas. He says not only does he enjoy it, but it's the only way he can think of to get even with the Italians.

Marty Goodfellow called and asked how I was doing. I'm glad he didn't ask what. After reassuring this weaselly little bastard that everything was fine, I took to my bed for my daily nap and my daily conversation with my Maker, both of which I believed contributed to my well-being and peace of mind.

After the Lord's Prayer, which it seems I've been saying since the womb, I began my one-sided (so far) conversa-

tion with God. First, I asked for blessings for those near
and dear to me starting with my darling little Reiko, and
my two little angel boys, Bobby and Timothy. Bobby is
rapidly outgrowing the angel-boy stage and graduating
into the wise-ass age, but as Ma Barker used to say,
"There's no such thing as a bad boy," so I haven't used
the thumbscrews on him yet. After Reiko, Bobby and
Timothy, I ask for blessings for an almost endless list of
all my devoted animals, going back to my first dog,
twelve-year-old Laddie, a lovable little Scottish Terrier,
who was born on the same day that I was, and who
dashing about with joy at the prospect of a ride in our
Willys-Overland, which my father was backing out of
the garage, was crushed under one of the wheels. I still
have that picture in my mind—that little black dog lying
where we had placed him, in the shade of an old oak,
breathing his last, and trying desperately to wag his tail to
tell us it was all right. My father cried and I don't believe
he ever got over this tiny tragedy. Whenever we spoke of
little Laddie in the years that followed, I thought I could
see the beginning of tears in his gentle gray eyes.

I have never missed a day asking God to keep *all* of my
animals happy forever in the Happy Hunting Ground
where animals are supposed to go. And there is such a list
of them: cats, Lizzie (a male, so named by my Aunt
Gladys—apparently I was too young to know why), and
Siki, a shiny black one, who was named after Battling
Siki, the famous Senegalese boxer of long ago who moved
like a lovely black cat in the ring. Anthony and Cleopatra,
our twin dachshunds, who used to sleep in my crotch until
that fatal Christmas night, when Patsy, as we called Cleopatra, died under the bed, where she had found safety
from the fire which leveled our house. I asked a special
blessing for her. Then there were Jack and Jill, who were
rabbits who thought they were people (they ate at the
table with us). There was Tito, a tiny canary, who was
named after Tito Schipa, the Metropolitan chap—not
Tito, the Yugoslavian chap. There are so many wonderful
dogs—Freddie, Peggy, Peter the I, Peter the II, Angus,
Chinook, Dutchess, Eric, and Gertrude. Gertrude, I think,

might have been the most dog of all. She was pure mutt and had more love for me than I knew what to do with. She had just wandered onto our California ranch one day and would not leave. I had a special prayer for her, too. We also had Bantam chickens led by a feisty little cock we called David because he thought he was a giant killer, and he might have been, but we didn't give him a chance. I asked God to bless our flock of tiny ducklings, who met an untimely end under the huge feet of Peter the Great (his full name), a Great Dane, who in play hopped over the fence into their coop and quite inadvertently stepped on the entire flock. I was sick at this—but for the simple precaution of placing a piece of chicken wire over the top of the pen, they would have lived.

I also asked blessings for my brother's precious little dachshund, Cappy, and other people's pets and the animals I see lying still on the many roads I've driven over in my life. This sounds a little on the odd side, but my compassion for the defenseless creatures of this world borders on the fanatic.

Also, I had quite a session with God about Tanuki, the first wolf I ever owned. Tanuki was a 150-pound Montana timber wolf and one of the loveliest creatures I have ever seen. His amber-colored eyes were soft and full of expression, and contrary to the belief that a wolf will never look you straight in the eye or at a camera, I found this not to be true at all. Tanuki looked at me directly and with great love. The facial expressions of wolves are much more pronounced than dogs and every mood is manifested in many subtle and delightful ways. Tanuki's demeanor was mostly one of great joy and the lust for living. Every day seemed to him like the greatest day on earth. I think I loved this happy animal almost as much as I loved my family because he was one of the family.

On the day we left Lost Lake for California a terrible scene ensued when I attempted to get Tanuki into a barred shipping crate, which was to go with us on the same 747 from Toronto. Tanuki, wary, then fearful, fought off any move I made to drag, push and pull him into the confines of the crate. After the first few times, he backed off

into a corner and bared his fangs and growled and
snarled, at the same time uttering an almost plaintive whine.
He was begging me to leave him alone and at the same
time warning me that he would slash me with his saberlike
canine teeth if I persisted in tormenting him—because
that's just what I was doing. His whole life had been spent
in tremendously large runs, or he was allowed to run free
on one of our islands, when the island was surrounded by
water and not ice; so when I suddenly started to put him
into the frighteningly small shipping crate, he was panic-
stricken.

My heart was torn by what I had to do, but I had no
choice. For a moment, during this terrible confrontation, I
was tempted to just open the steel mesh gate and let him
race off into the woods, but I knew he could never make
it on his own. If he didn't starve to death, he would have
probably been set upon by the native wild wolves because
he didn't belong. Whichever way, he would die, so by
much chicanery and soft talk I managed to get a strong
choke chain around his neck, and Charlie Burke, Reiko,
Bobby and I dragged him through the opening of the shipping crate by means of a hole cut in the other end. I have
never seen an animal struggle like this, and when we got
him inside and slammed the crate door shut, he just col-
lapsed on the floor of the crate and lay there, without
moving, his eyes wide-open in abject terror.

It took me almost an hour before I was calm enough to
help with the loading of the luggage and our other animals, which included another wolf, an Alaskan timber
wolf, who at eight months old was bigger and stronger
than Tanuki but much more tractable, when it came to
shipping crates anyway. He entered his like he had done
it every day.

When Charlie Burke nosed his Cessna 180 into the dock
at Chinookville, and a couple of boys started to unload it,
one of them called, "Hey, Jack, come here." He was
standing beside the just-unloaded crate containing Tanuki.
As I walked over to him, I knew Tanuki was dead. I
looked inside the crate and he was lying just as he had fall-
en after we dragged him into it. He hadn't moved, and

blood was running from his mouth. The struggle had been too much. His great heart had burst.

"Reiko," I said, "you take the kids and the luggage and the other animals out to the airport. I'm going back to Lost Lake with Tanuki."

Reiko said nothing but her eyes were full of tears. Bobby who was old enough to know what was going on was too busy running around the dock after Timothy who was too young to understand.

Charlie Burke flew me and Tanuki, now wrapped in a Hudson Bay blanket, back to Lost Lake. I lifted the now-stiffening body of Tanuki into a canoe and picked up a shovel and pickax from the tool shed and paddled out to the island where he had romped and played and made believe he was hunting all during the long sunny days of two summers. And where he would stalk me like he was trailing a moose, then suddenly burst from under the bushes to make playful slashes at my legs—just grazing the skin. Or he in turn would get the same treatment from Pussycat, the cougar, who played these games a little more seriously and sometimes was forced to leap halfway up a tree to get away from Tanuki's resentful counterattack.

When I reached the island, I lifted Tanuki from the canoe, and then I had to sit down and rest for a moment. The tree I sat under was one under which I had whiled away many a dreamy summer's day after a romp with Tanuki. I would sit with his great and lovely head in my lap, scratching behind his ears, and once in a while he would take my hand between his powerful jaws and gently press it. The way a wolf shows his love.

Suddenly I started to cry at the terrible injustice of it all! Why hadn't he been born to roam the great forests? Free, instead of being caged as a pet? Why did I have to kill him? For kill him I did, just as surely as if I had shot him.

It took a long time to bury Tanuki in the rocky soil of his little island, but finally the job was done. And afterward, I knelt down beside this lonely grave and prayed.

I don't know how long I knelt beside Tanuki's grave,

but gradually I became aware that it was snowing—gently and silently—and before long Tanuki's last resting place was completely obliterated. Now there was only a white mantle covering everything. It was like he had never existed. But he had.

"Good-bye, Tanuki," I said. From the deep forest which surrounded Lost Lake came the long, low howl of a wild wolf. It was coincidence, but for a moment I thought it was Tanuki. Maybe it was.

8

WORKING for Johnny Blackwell was like being a stroke on a Roman slave barge in the year 14 B.C. (which wasn't a very good year for this particular occupation). There was one difference. You weren't chained to your oar, but you were more or less tied to your telephone. The telephone was mostly used to announce "meetings," which were endless, pointless, and supernumerous.

The "meetings" were held at a fanciful place called the Johnny Blackwell Building. The office was upstairs over Johnny Blackwell's "Blowhole," a nautical type drinking place designed by Mr. Muff, the Sunset Strip's most celebrated interior decorator, to look like the inside of a whale, complete with entrails, which were indirectly lighted and hung from the ceiling by invisible wires. The whole effect would make unwary tourists gasp in horror, but they crowded the place night after night, hoping to see their idol, Johnny Blackwell.

Dino's was just down the street and was also crowded with people from as far away as Glendale drooling over the possibility that they might catch a glimpse of Dean Martin, who in its ten or so years of operation has never been near the place, but the operators of this trap keep hinting that Dino's is like Dean Martin's second home, which of course is one of Sunset Strip's big jokes. His *first* home isn't even like his second home.

The Johnny Blackwell meetings always started out with anywhere from an hour to a two-hour wait for him. I never waited for more than a half hour. This marked me lousy in his book, but finally he did start to show more or less on time. He would arrive with his shadow, Marty

73

Goodfellow, his sidewinder manager, and two or three
girls whom Johnny was going to use in his next picture
and as much as he could *before* then. The girls were told
to wait in the outer office where Miss Zooker, the recep-
tionist, spent her long, lonely days unsnarling her J. C.
Penney wig and auditioning nail polish.

The conference room was wallpapered with some kind
of cheap black velvet wallpaper, giving the illusion that we
were discussing comedy from inside a deluxe coffin. The
deadening sound effects of the wallpaper and the heavy
drapes made every word spoken seem to fall from the
mouth into a bottomless pit. There was no resonance. No
inflection and no laughing.

I was surprised and happy to see Marve Froman at one
of these first meetings. Marve was an old friend from the
days of radio and an extremely talented writer with an in-
cisive mind, plus the quiet ability to make the most insulting remarks about everything and anything that needed
this kind of treatment. He was the ideal man to have
aboard the rescue team, which would be required to save
any pictorial project from the cockeyed machinations of
Blackwell and Goodfellow.

Marve hadn't the slightest compunction about telling
any actor, director or producer that he was a cretin, but
his delivery was so underplayed that his opponents (which
they all were) never became upset. They didn't seem to
realize that they had been stabbed until they started to
bleed internally. By this time Marty would be inquiring
into the health of his victim's lovely family. And sending
his best.

There were two other writers, who seemed to have been
hired for their ability to nod their heads, which they did
continuously. They never contributed a word, and for all
the world knew, they were deaf-mutes, although they did
endow these morbid gatherings with a variety of noncom-
mittal grunts.

The Devil and the Hot Virgin was discussed for hours.
That is, this epic was discussed by Johnny and Marty,
while Marve and I and the two zombies sat around like

attentive wax dummies and wished we were downstairs in the whale's guts—getting loaded.

Marty Goodfellow's main theme always seemed to be that Johnny Blackwell didn't need writers because he was such a great ad-libber. The two zombies nodded every time he reiterated this while Marve Froman looked attentive, making him the greatest actor of all time.

On the surface, the ability to ad-lib would not seem too important in the making of a motion picture. Improvisation as a rule was frowned upon by directors, producers, and writers, and the other actors in the scene, but in the case of comedians, sometimes it was an asset and could improve a scene, or at least make it seem less deadly after about twenty takes. This was one of the great tricks of the Old Master, Bob Hope. Bob would wait until everybody on the movie set—the director, the assistants, the grips, the cameramen, the script girl, and everyone else—was so sick and tired of hearing and seeing the same comedic bit they were ready to scream with irritation and boredom; then he would change one of the lines to a new and fresh one, and the whole crew would break up laughing. The director would scream, "Bob! That's marvelous! Oh, Bob! Keep that in! It's marvelous!" And the line would stay. The line that Bob had so carefully waited until just the right moment to slip in, of course, had been concocted the night before at his house, where gag sessions with his writers (of which I was one) were nightly held in preparation for the next day's shooting.

This clever bit of strategy, which no other comic had thought of before, made him the man to watch in his earlier movies and enabled him to come to Hollywood prominence in a much shorter time than his contemporaries. A truly remarkable man, this Hope—a thinking comedian. Very rare.

Johnny Blackwell's great ad-libbing ability, which should have been an asset in a comedy movie, unfortunately was not strictly off the top of Johnny Blackwell's head, as Marty Goodfellow had been propagandizing for years, but the end result of many hours of carefully conjured-up comedy by highly paid writers. Not that it mattered much, so long as writers are highly paid, but the day-after-day insistence that Johnny Blackwell comes up with *all* this marvelous material just by spouting off when called upon makes the highly paid writers look like vampire bats who are just hanging around long enough to blood-suck him dry. Not a very nice picture when you notice other parents edging their children away from you at PTA meetings.

As Marty Goodfellow droned on, though he was praising Johnny's great ability, even Johnny wasn't paying too much attention. Marty's comedic proposals almost always ran to transvestitism. To Marty, there was nothing funnier than Johnny dressed as an old lady with definite nymphomaniac manifestations.

"Anybody can put on women's clothes," Marty would say. "But if it's an old lady who wants to get balled, you got real comedy."

"Yeah," Marve, who was semiconscious, agreed. "Real comedy."

"How about making her an airline hostess?" I said, which is exactly what Johnny had portrayed just the week before, on his regular television show.

"Great!" Marty said, pained that he had been forced to agree with a writer. "She can suck around Rock Hudson—we got him set for the *Devil and the Hot Virgin.* Rock can be on the plane and Johnny can keep asking him, 'Coffee, tea or me?' "

"Yeah," said Johnny, who suddenly stopped sniffing under his arm to see if his Right Guard was working. "Coffee, tea or me? That's funny. I thought about that line last night when I was in bed."

"That was the title of a book—it came out a couple of years ago," I had to say. "It was written by a couple of airline hostesses—"

"Book writers!" Marty said. "What the hell do they know?"

"Yeah," I said, "it isn't like a movie. Where you can ad-lib."

"Johnny is one of the best ad-libbers in the business," Marty quickly said.

"We all *know* that," I said. "But we'll have to write something for Rock Hudson. Maybe he can't ad-lib too good, without Doris Day around."

"That's a minor detail which will work itself out," Marty said.

"Yeah," Johnny said, "don't worry about Rock—we play golf together all the time."

"What the hell's that got to do with a television movie about a horny old-lady airline hostess?"

"Nothing," Johnny said.

"Johnny's right," Marty said.

"Yeah," Marve said, "Johnny's right."

"Of course he is," Marty said, then in an aside to his meal ticket, "Johnny, they want you to appear on the *Tom Jones Show.*"

"Who's he?" Johnny said.

"He's a singer," Marty said.

"What's his Nielsen rating?"

"Well, not so good"—Marty could see his ten percent evaporating before his very eyes. "The last time I checked he was in seventy-sixth place."

"Fuck 'em," Johnny said.

"I'll make a note of that," Marty said.

"Is the meeting over?" I said.

"Oh, yes," Marty said, glancing for confirmation from Johnny, then getting it. "Yes, the meeting is over. Now you all know what you're supposed to do?" This was greeted by various grunts, none of them enthusiastic.

This was typical of a writers' meeting, or story conference, for Johnny Blackwell's big new movie. Nothing happened. It became more and more apparent to Marve and me that we would have to write this thing ourselves—away from the blue sky thinking of a roomful of supposedly creative people. Strange, but this has always happened—we are supposed to be writing a scenario for a movie, but not once does anyone ever sit down at the typewriter and type.

"What are we gonna do with *The Devil and the Hot Virgin?*" I asked Marve.

"Well," Marve said, "whatever we do with it, let's type it on a roll of long thin paper—this will give it some practical value."

9

PEOPLE in California live a different kind of life. I'm sure you've heard this before, but it's true. For instance, when they get out of bed in the morning, they don't rush to the kitchen to pour themselves a glass of orange juice. Mainly because they don't know what orange juice is. They think an orange is a gay apple. The last California orange tree died in 1946—just one year after the invasion started. The invaders were from back East and they did less for the splendid California orange groves than the Tasmanian fruit fly. These invaders, or migrants, if you're kind, took one look at the miles and miles of lovely California hills, valleys, orange groves, redwood groves, lakes, mountains and rivers and immediately visualized how these unprogressive areas would look covered by housing developments, liquor stores, supermarkets, filling stations, and drive-in urinals. This last is something new in Art Linkletter Enterprises. This man, Art Linkletter, is a business genius. More about this remarkable man in my next Book-of-the-Month Club selection. Also, more about the fascinating item appearing in the April 22, 1970 issue of the New York *Daily News* movie column; "Heart transplant surgeon Christiaan Barnard will make his movie debut this summer in a picture with Arlene Dahl. Barnard will portray a surgeon who performs heart surgery on Arlene with the result that she falls in love with him. Arlene will sing in the picture" (during the operation?). I'd like to know more about this myself. The next time I hear Arlene sing, I'll stop the music and ask her.

Other differences in California living, of which there are many compared with people who live in, say, Omaha, Nebraska. The good citizens of Omaha, Nebraska, would never think of taking a dip in their swimming pools in mid-January, which, as I write, turns out to be true also in California. In Omaha, Nebraska, you'd freeze your ass off, as would happen in California—only in California the process wouldn't take quite so long. I'd say that in less than five minutes you'd hear a loud metallic "bonk! bonk!" and that would be your buttocks hitting the pavement, unless you have the new silent buttocks developed by Du Pont ("Better living through chemistry").

The house we rented for our Hollywood stay was in Roxbury Hills, where, strangely enough, you could still hear the mad yipping of coyotes during the night. They hadn't the sense to know, apparently, that coyotes were through in that part of the world. Coyotes haven't gotten the word anywhere: from all reports, they are *increasing* in numbers, which is really reversing the trend. They are not only not endangered. *We* are. But enough for the moment about the last courageous Americans. Let's get back to our life in Hollywood.

Reiko loved the Farmer's Market, which hasn't seen a farmer in at least thirty years. She liked it because you could buy everything you didn't need there. Anything from a toucan to matched "his" and "hers" jockstraps, for football players who weren't too sure what they wanted to be when they grew up.

I liked the Farmer's Market in bygone days when I was young and not gay in Hollywood because it was a great place to meet would-be starlets who had just gotten off the bus from Sioux City and wanted to be discovered by a big movie producer. I used to carry my light meter, when I hung around there, testing the various lighting conditions. These future carhops wouldn't know what a light meter was, but I wore puttees and a monocle and my cap on backward so they knew I had something to do with the motion picture industry—and frankly, I did—I saw every movie that Noah Beery, Jr., ever made.

Even with the elaborate trap I had set up for these star-struck neophytes, I must admit I never had much luck with them. They always wanted to meet Darryl Zanuck, and they would simply not believe that he was up in my apartment waiting for me to bring him some undiscovered talent. So far as I was concerned, most of the time, I never got to discover whether they had any talent either. In any direction. I think I would have done better in Sioux City just hanging around the bowling alley, or the Empire State Building, picking up some of King Kong's discards. They might be a wee-bit hysterical, but more's the fun.

The school where Bobby was supposed to learn a thing or two about education was something else again. Not only did they not pledge allegiance to the flag or say a prayer, but if they raised their hands to go to the bathroom, it had to be with the closed fist.

Apparently there was no dope problem at this school. You could buy all you wanted. And the whole educational system, typical or not of California, seemed to be far in advance of progressive. The school bus had a bar in it. This last according to Mrs. Sonnabend, a neighbor, who had a son who always came home loaded from kindergarten. I asked her why she didn't go to school and complain, and she said she would have but her son was the bartender and the only kid in kindergarten who knew anything about mixed drinks.

The report cards from Bobby's new California school did not contain any A's, B's, C's, or D's—they contained "Excellent," "Satisfactory," "Could do better," and "Forget it." Bobby seemed to be somewhere between "Could do better" and "Forget it," so I made an appointment with his teacher—a Mrs. Alma Binch—and promptly at 3:15 one Friday afternoon I was sitting opposite this normal-school graduate, wondering whether she was "Excellent," "Satisfactory," "Could do better," or "Forget it"—my almost immediate conclusion was "Forget it." Mrs. Alma Binch looked exactly like her name. She was rail-thin. Where her bust should have been there were twin dimples. I thought she could at least have worn a pump-up brassiere—after all, most schools are pushing sex education and this would have at least made the average boy-child aware that there are gradients—gender speaking. Mrs. Alma Binch in her present depressed condition could have been

Arnold Stang, which would have been an improvement.
Her Ben Franklin eyeglasses were not just her gesture
toward the present-day fad, I'm sure. She also had something else that was not going for her and those were her
legs. I thought at first she was wearing panty hose that
had once belonged to Tony Galento, but I was wrong.
These were her legs, which I'm sure were slightly rippling
every time the air conditioner surged a bit.

Almost at once Mrs. Binch and I were at loggerheads,
as they say in the Little Golden Book of overworked
clichés.

"Bobby seems to be having a problem here, Mrs.
Binch," I said in my most winning tone.

"What do you expect?" Mrs. Binch said, chopping off
her words like a snapping turtle with a bad bite. "The
schools back East are nowhere near up to *our* academic
level."

"What about Harvard, Yale and Princeton?" I said, immediately realizing that I had picked the wrong three
schools.

"I am referring to grade schools," she said, nipping off
just the teeniest bit of her nose. "Your son cannot add, sub-
tract, multiply, read nor write with any degree of effi-
ciency—compared to the children who have been with us
since the beginning." I didn't know whether she meant the
beginning of time or just the Ice Age, but I let it go for
the moment.

"I thought he was getting along fine," I said.

"You Eastern people are all alike," Mrs. Binch said.
"You're all too busy with your own problems to find out
anything about what your children are like. Where was
your son last night at ten o'clock?"

"He was in bed," I said.

"Are you sure?"

"Yes, I'm sure. He was sleeping right next to me—between his little brother and his mother."

Mrs. Binch's nose arched. "All four of you in the same
bed?"

"Yes," I said, "it's an old Japanese custom."

Mrs. Binch's nose arched more and her nostrils flared

to the point of being obscene. "You're *Japanese?*" Her tone suggested I'd better not deny it so I didn't.

"Look," I said, "what's the principal's name?"

"Mr. Binch," she said. "He's my husband. Do you wish to go over my head and speak with him?" Her jaws were really snapping now and her nose had taken to nervously ducking.

"I don't want to go over anyone's head," I said. "But if my son is going to become President, I think he should have *some* education and——"

This started things into high gear.

"That's the trouble with you Americans," she said, "always shooting for the top! Who's going to do the dirty jobs——like sweeping the streets, pumping out the septic tanks, tuning up the computers?"

"I don't know," I said. "That's up to the unions——they take care of things like that."

"Not anymore they don't," Mrs. Binch said. "We're organizing, and all the dirty jobs are going to be taken care of by the people who have the clean jobs now!"

"What does that mean?" I said. "That sounds slightly—— er——liberal."

"Why don't you want to legalize pot?" Mrs. Binch countered. "You have your booze——why can't we have pot?"

"So far as I'm concerned," I said, "they can legalize anything——including the Democrats. I don't think it's going to make the slightest difference."

"Do you think I should be entitled to an abortion?" Mrs. Binch said.

"Why not?" I said. "I have my booze."

"You're confusing me," she said.

"I'm sorry."

"How about Karl Marx?"

"He's buried in a London cemetery. The last time I was in England I took a tour and visited his grave——it's real cute."

"Are you queer?" Mrs. Binch said.

"Mrs. Binch," I said, touching up my lipstick, "I came here to talk about my son, Bobby."

"Oh, yes," she said, "the retarded child."

"He's not retarded," I said, feeling my gorge rise, my hackles rise and my voice lower. "It's the California school system that's retarded! Why can't *Johnny* read? Because the *teachers* can't. When was the last time you read a book?"

Mrs. Bench was not taken back by my change of mien. She looked me straight and said, "I have *never* read a book. I read synopses."

"Well," I said, "I've never heard anything like that before—not from a schoolteacher anyway."

"Let's be realistic," Mrs. Binch said, removing her Ben Franklin spectacles and tapping them alongside her now-relaxed nose. "If I wasted my time reading, how on earth would I ever find the time to protest?"

"Protest against what?"

"Books."

"Mrs. Binch," I said, "you've defeated me. Completely."

"That was my intention," she said. "Now, would you care for a martini?" Smiling (I think), she touched a button and a junior bar sprang from within her large oaken desk and stopped with a merry clink of bottles and glasses.

"I'd love one," I said, "but I've got a lot of broken watches to fix this afternoon and I need every bit of steadiness I have."

"Well," she said, pausing for a moment in the creation of the world's strongest martini, "to each his own"—a bottle of Gilbey's suspended in midair. "Do you know who said that?"

"Who?" I said.

"My husband," she said. "He masturbates a lot."

"And he's the principal of the school?" I said.

"He's also an Aztec god," she said.

And that was the day Bobby was transferred to a private school run by nuns and the ROTC. I felt that there he might be in danger of becoming a general or a priest, but never an alcoholic, masturbating liberal—which might be fun, but it'll never sell insurance or used cars.

10

THE days were growing shorter and more gruesome as the script deadline for *The Devil and the Hot Virgin* was screaming down on us. We had more and more nonproductive meetings in Johnny Blackwell's black hole of Calcutta, as we were now calling it.

We had two new writers. I never found out their names, but they looked like they had been created by Botticelli for a mural on the wall of a Sicilian post office. Maybe they weren't writers—maybe they were enforcers hired by Frederico Fellucio, an Italian producer, who suddenly appeared on the scene, at the insistence of Marty and Johnny, to take complete charge of the production of *The Devil and the Hot Virgin,* and if Marve and I didn't shape up, we would be found tied together in a storm drain with a couple of shots through our heads.

"I hope," Marve whispered confidentially, "if they shoot me through the head, they miss my gold earring."

"What would it matter?" I confidentially whispered back.

"It would matter a great deal," Marve said. "I promised it to my eldest son—he's thinking seriously of studying at UCLA to become a queer."

"What the hell are you two whispering about?!" Marty yelled. "You workin' for somebody else while we're try'na get a story here?"

"On the contrary," Marve said, "I was just trying out a new thought on Jack. How would it be if we changed the title from *The Devil and the Hot Virgin* to *Irving and Sandra and Terence and Moira?*"

"Why?" snapped Johnny.

"Yeah, why?" Marty, a split snap behind Johnny, snapped.

"Because," Marve said, "it sounds dirty and also a little like *The Cohens and the Kellys* and *Abie's Irish Rose,* which were very successful."

"It also sounds like *Bob and Carol and Ted and Alice,*" Johnny said.

"That's the idea," Marve said. "Capture the spirit of the times."

"Yeah," I said, because I felt something was expected of me.

"Translation," Miss Zooker, Johnny's secretary said, "if one movie makes it big, do another one exactly like it."

Marve kissed Miss Zooker full on the lips, which proved what a gutsy bastard he was, and in his loudest but most carefully modulated voice said, "Miss Zooker, you're a beautiful human being!" Then to Johnny, "Johnny, you've got a gem here—don't ever lose her. Now, *who* can we get to play *Irving?*"

Before Johnny or Marty or Fellucio or Miss Zooker or the two hoodlum-writers could jump in, Marve was off and running. "How about Barbra Streisand? She'd be the *perfect* Irving!"

"How are you gonna get her?" I said. "She costs too much—besides, she's difficult. When they made *Dolly* she was always fighting with Gene Kelly."

"Then how about Gene Kelly for Irving?" Marve said.

"No," I said, "he doesn't wanna dance anymore. He wants to direct. He wants to hang up his dancing shoes."

"I *like* that!" Miss Zooker said, emboldened by her earlier success. "Hang up his dancing shoes. That's got the whole poignant history of show business in five little words—'Hang up his dancing shoes'—lovely, lovely, *lovely.*"

"Look, Miss Zooker," Marve said, in a sotto voce drill sergeant tone, "this is not a dancing picture—"

"But you said—" Miss Zooker said, suddenly contrite under her Jewish-Afro hairdo.

"I'm a writer," Marve said. "I can say a lot of things

that just don't work out. Now let's get this straight—*Irving and Sandra and Terence and Moira* is a simple story about simple wife-swapping in an average, everyday, simple neighborhood."

Miss Zooker was not to go down so easily. "Couldn't they start out dancing," she said, "then wind up in the sack? Or start out in the sack and wind up dancing?"

"No," Marve said, "we'd have to hire a choreographer, and we don't have that kind of loot. This is a very low-budget picture. That's why we have to be more porno than graphic—if I may be clever for the moment."

"I may vomit," Johnny Blackwell said, causing all eyes to rivet on him—waiting.

"Please," Marve said after a moment, "Johnny, don't ever use that word again. I know this is your office and all that, but whenever I hear the word 'vomit,' it makes me wanna puke. Now, let's pull this story conference together, shall we? How about a nice clean picture with Doris Day and Dick Van Dyke?"

"Yeah," said Frederico Fellucio, coming to life and lighting a long thin Italian cigar that smelled like a burning ghat, "we could throw in Crosby as a priest and show it in monasteries—between vespers. A picture like that wouldn't make a dime!"

"What the hell is going on here?" Marty exploded. "Who the hell wants Doris Day and Dick Van Dyke in a picture that's got Johnny Blackwell?"

Marve turned to me, exposing his arrogant back to Marty, and said, "How about if Doris appeared topless?"

"I don't know," I said. "She might feel that that would louse up her image—unless, of course, we have a very good story reason—like Doris is a pioneer woman, alone in a little sod-roof hut in the middle of North Dakota, with two very hungry five-day-old babies and Doris keeps them from starving in the only way she knows?"

"Which way is that?" asked Miss Zooker.

"You'll never know," Marve said kindly.

"I like it," Fellucio said. "It has a nice Italian feeling—like *Stromboli*."

"I never tasted Stromboli," Miss Zooker said.

"I think we better terminate this meeting," Marty said, looking at Johnny for confirmation, but Johnny was busy flipping the pages of the new Playboy calendar.

"Maybe Doris would go for it if we gave the scene some good background music," Marve said, "like the Mormon Tabernacle Choir."

"Maybe Mick Jagger's got something that would fit," Miss Zooker contributed, drunk with her new power. "Now who can we get to play Irving?"

"What's the matter with Doris Day?" Marve said.

"What about the hungry babies?" I said. "And all that money pissed away on the Mormon Tabernacle Choir— and Mick Jagger? Besides, we've got to be realistic. Irving is a man!"

"Jesus Christ!" Marve said softly. "Details!"

"He's right, you know," Miss Zooker said, indicating me to Marve.

"How do you know?" Marve said. "We're the writers— Irving can be anything we want him to be. Might be a nice surprise twist if Irving turns out to be Joan Crawford."

"That don't hit me," Miss Zooker said, now acting as chairman of the board. "How about you, Jack?"

"I'm worried about the title," I said.

"Miss Zooker," Marty said, goosing her with his poached alligator hide shoe, "why don't you go for coffee?"

Miss Zooker completely ignored this request.

I continued, "I think we ought to change the title to something that will indicate to the buying public that this isn't just one of those run-of-the-mill sex pictures. We gotta elevate the title somehow—add some intellectual class. How about calling it *Irving and Sandra and Terence and Moira and War and Peace?*"

"I like it," Frederico Fellucio said.

"Might work," Marve said. "An awful lot of people are just crazy for Tolstoy."

"Who's he?" Miss Zooker wanted to know.

"He used to go to school with Dmitri Tiomkin," Marve

said, "but he's a great writer. He took the Moscow phone book and made an eight-hour movie out of it."

"I think we're going off on too much of a tangent," Miss Zooker said, lighting one of Fellucio's cigars. "We want to make *Irving and Sandra and Terence and Moira* a simple, straightforward, sweet, wholesome, wife-swapping story."

"You mean like *Gentle Ben?*" Marve said.

"*Gentle Ben* is about a bear," Marty said with great authority.

"He's right, you know," Miss Zooker said.

"There's an idea," Marve said. "How about a bear-swapping story—Disney'll buy that in a minute. All we need is a little cruelty and the casting is easy—Doris Day and Dick Van Dyke. Or Joi Lansing."

"Joi Lansing might be good for Sandra," I said, trying to be practical.

"You mean instead of Irving?" Marve said.

"You got a dirty mind, Marve," I said. "This is a wife-swapping story—nothing more. Irving and Sandra and Terence and Moira got to get into bed together very innocently and naturally. We don't want anything contrived."

"Somebody should contrive a story for *The Devil and the Hot Virgin,*" Frederico Fellucio said. "I come all the way from Italy to make a movie for America and what do I get? Gentle Ben in bed with Doris Day—"

"You weren't paying attention," Marve said, then, "How about we have Irving and Sandra and Terence and Moira inside a spaceship—on their way to Mars? They get bored and the next thing they know they're in the hay with each other's wives."

"That's contrived," Johnny said, looking up from the Playboy calendar.

"I know," Marve said. "I just contrived it."

"I think it's marvelous," Miss Zooker said, flipping her cigar ash into Fellucio's lap. "I can just see the big scene—they're all weightless—weightless and nude. Just think of the fun we can have with them just trying to grab each other."

Johnny dropped the Playboy calendar and started to listen to the story conference.

"Yeah," Marve said, "but the girls will have a big advantage."

"That's clever," Miss Zooker said, "but we need something besides cleverness—we gotta have blood. How we gonna get some blood in this film? Did you see *M*A*S*H?*"

"Yeah," Marv said.

"What'd you think?" Miss Zooker said.

"It needed blood," Marve said.

"Exactly," Miss Zooker said. "Now, in our picture Irving gets bit by a rabid cobra."

"Beautiful," Marve said.

"A rabid cobra!" Marty squeaked, his face growing more and more purple as this insane conference continued. "How the hell did a rabid cobra get inside a spaceship on the way to Mars?"

"That's easy," Marve said, in his most irritatingly silky-smooth tone. "At the last minute, just before lift-off at Cape Kennedy, Irving gets a box lunch from his mother plainly marked 'Chicken soup for Irving.' But—now listen carefully—his mother didn't send it at all."

"Who did?" Marty said, and he really wanted to know.

"A man,"—Marve's tone grew sinister—"known all over the Middle East as a double agent."

"Yeah," Miss Zooker said, enthralled. "Say, this thing is really beginning to shape up, isn't it? Marty, why don't you go for coffee? Make mine black."

Marty was so taken off guard by this direct order, he said, "Okay."

"I'll go with you," Frederico Fellucio said.

"So will I," Johnny Blackwell said, and the three left—followed by the two hoodlum-writers, or whatever they were. I never found out.

"Well," Marve said, "it worked. We got rid of those jerks. Maybe this will put a stop to these idiotic meetings or story conferences or what the hell ever they are called and we can get some work done."

"I don't like it," Miss Zooker said, her eyes glazed with

the fierce intensity of a scientist just about to unlock the mystery of the universe.

"You don't like what?" Marve said.

"We started out," Miss Zooker said, in a voice that sounded far away, "with a sweet, simple, heartwarming story about wife-swapping, and now what have we got? A big international Harold Robbins type of worldwide intrigue. The public won't buy it! Harold Robbins is too clean!"

"What about Jackie Susann?" Marve asked.

"What about Jack E. Leonard?" I asked.

"Picture, if you will," Miss Zooker said softly, "picture, if you will, a small sleepy little New England village in the year 1678. It's Deerfield, Massachusetts. It's a quiet little town."

"Too quiet," Marve said.

"Exactly," Miss Zooker said. "It's too quiet because Deerfield, Massachusetts, is surrounded by five thousand bloodthirsty savage Indians and is about to get massacred."

"Miss Zooker," I said, "Marve and I were just having fun before and——"

Miss Zooker was not to be dissuaded. "Picture, if you will——"

"What about Irving and Sandra and Terence and Moira?" Marve interrupted.

"They are holed up," Miss Zooker said, "if you'll forgive the choice of words, inside the Deerfield fort, which is supposed to protect Deerfield from the attack of five thousand bloodthirsty savage Indians, and they won't let anyone else inside the fort—and this is the inside story of how Deerfield, Massachusetts, got massacred in the year 1678 because nobody could get into the fort to get their guns to fight off the Indian attack."

"Gee," Marve said, "you know what Miss Zooker has got here? She's got a sit-mass."

"What the hell is that?" I said.

"A situation massacre," Marve said. "Might start a whole new trend. It's *exciting*. That's the word—'*exciting!*'"

"That's the word that everybody in Hollywood uses

when they're not too sure of something," I said, then to Miss Zooker: "Miss Zooker, I have to ask you something—"

"Anything at all, Jackie baby," Miss Zooker said, smiling through the tears of creativity.

"It's this—why were Irving and Sandra and Terence and Moira swapping wives during an Indian massacre?"

"Oh, that's easy," Miss Zooker said, lighting two cigarettes, like Charles Boyer did once, and smoking both of them herself. "*They* don't know it was an Indian massacre. They thought all that screaming outside was ecstasy. They thought everybody in Deerfield, Massachusetts, was wife-swapping. And as it turns out—and here's our denouement—they *are*—it's not a massacre at all. And for a finish, just before the final fade-out, we take a wide-angle shot of everybody in Deerfield, Massachusetts—five hundred and seventy-three wife-swapping couples—humping their way up and over the lovely Berkshire Hills toward the picturesque little village of Plymouth, Vermont, arriving just in time for the Easter sunrise services at Calvin Coolidge's grave—it's like a rally."

"I like that last," Marve said, "but it may be *too* much. What about the code? What about Jack Valenti?"

"Sensational," Miss Zooker whooped. "Why didn't we think of this before—he's the *perfect* Irving!"

Thus the meeting ended. It had accomplished nothing so far as *The Devil and the Hot Virgin* was concerned, but it did confuse Marty Goodfellow, Johnny Blackwell, and Frederico Fellucio, and it also scared them a little. From that day on, they treated Marve and me, and also Miss Zooker, with a bit more respect—even if it was only the kind of respect usually reserved for potentially violent psychopaths. From that day on, they were careful not to say or do anything that would trigger us into running amuck, physically or orally.

11

THE Hollywood scene is dominated by parties or, I should say, party givers. They came in all sizes and shapes and from all levels of the economic strata. The wife of a Hollywood plumber had outdoor barbecues in her backyard with a guest list of other Hollywood plumbers and their wives, or girlfriends or in some cases, with older plumbers—both.

The Hollywood caste system, which has been spoken and written of ad nauseum is still very much in effect. A $1,000,000-per-movie actor wouldn't be caught dead with a $750,000-per-movie actress, unless, of course, her super-breasts warranted his slumming a bit.

The first party to which Reiko and I were invited was given by Mrs. Custer, who was celebrating the 96th anniversary of the general's miscalculation at the Little Big Horn. I can't swear that it was Mrs. Custer or what it was she was celebrating, but in the garbled introductions, that's what it sounded like.

The party was held at Mrs. Custer's palatial mansion in the Rosenkrantz Estates section of Holmby Hills. Her home was one of the oldest in the area, having been completed more than four months before. As you drove up the long winding driveway, between rows of stately dead eucalyptus trees, Mrs. Custer's Rosenkrantz Estates home with its stately white, fluted columns across the front of the lovely early-Spanish ranch house made it look like a Puerto Rican Mount Vernon—with a dash of Holiday Inn. And the lighting of the grounds with its color wheels and flashing bulbs exuded the carefree insouciance of Roseland Ballroom. At any moment I half expected to see a waltz

contest followed by the presentation of cups by Lawrence
Welk. Mrs. Custer seemed to have a thing for the famous
statue of the "winged victory of Samothrace." The lawns
were covered with this statuary. There must have been
fifty or sixty copies of this work dotting the landscape almost as far as the eye could see. I could visualize Mrs.
Custer, who was wealthy enough to do it, deciding one
day that a change of scene would be nice and suddenly
clapping her hands and her whole Rosenkrantz Estates
ménage would fly down to Acapulco, leaving nothing but
an enormous crater in the center of the Rosenkrantz Estates to be filled by Mr. Rosenkrantz with a difficult polo
field, or leveled to be used as a training ground for future
unwed mothers (a nice soft turf could be arranged) as
long as divots were replaced.

Reiko and I arrived more or less on time and we were
given a royal reception. This was the first and last royal
reception we were to receive in Hollywood and was
prompted by the typical Hollywood attitude toward celeb-
rities. They couldn't quite place us, but they knew they'd
seen us before, and rather than take a chance on not
being friendly to someone who might be important, most
of the guests, who all looked like Gene Barry or Pamela
Tiffin, greeted us like we had just come by yacht.

This gathering, as all Hollywood gatherings, was gener-
ously sprinkled by a large representation of eyeglassed
gnomes who were Hollywood agents. Or flesh peddlers, as
they were known at Swift and company, where they occa-
sionally did business with their dog and cat food department (when an actor got too tough to sell to the movies).

The regalia at the party was unbelievable. Lace and
costume jewelry and multiple rings were *de rigueur*. Every
actor was a ruffed Sir Walter Raleigh and every actress
was wearing long pants. A chicken sexer would have gone
mad trying to make a decision. Very few guests had their
own hair. The men wore Prince Valiant wigs and the women had dark curls (if they were white—straight blond if
they were black).

There were a few token teen-agers to keep within the
Fair Practices Act, but most of the superstars were over

the hill—or else it was chic to look like something from *Death Valley Days*. These stars were over the hill geriatrically but not financially. Most of them had bought California real estate when it had trees on it instead of used car lots. This wasn't by any particularly brilliant foresight on the part of the child stars (and that's all they ever were even into their eighties); all property in those days came in large chunks, and if you wanted an acre or two to build a house, you had to take the rest of the land that went with it, which sometimes amounted to 50 or more acres. Which was nice to own, if it just happened to be in the Wilshire district.

"Oh, there you are!" gushed someone, whom I presumed to be the hostess. "So glad you could come! Your last picture was marvelous!" My last picture had been as a Busby Berkeley boy in 1932, and it had been marvelous, so I said, "Thank you, it was a pleasure working with Eddie Cantor."

"Oh, yes," our Hostess said, "such a talent! How is he these days?"

"He's dead," I said.

"I'm so glad," our Hostess said. "I always say what good is money if you haven't got your health? Please give Eddie my best when you see him."

I promised I'd do just that, and I *will*, too.

Doug Shelby was at the party. Doug I had known since he was an agent. (Funny how so many Hollywoodians start out as agents. First they're lawyers, then they become agents and they switch to a more legitimate business.) Doug knew everybody in Hollywood. "Who's *that* over there?" I asked him, nodding toward a lovely girl who wore a backless evening gown with one cheek entirely exposed.

"Oh," Doug said, "some half-assed little starlet."

"Well put," I said.

"She used to live at Big Sur and play the guitar a lot," Doug said.

"Kim Novak lives at Big Sur," Reiko said. "She plays the guitar, too."

"Yeah," Doug said, "that's the thing nowadays. As soon

as you make it big in Hollywood you move as far as you can away from it and learn how to play the guitar. You learn folk dances, too."

"I wonder why," I said.

"What else you gonna do in Big Sur?" Doug said.

"Hump," I said crudely—but showing a deep insight into human nature.

"I'll bet they never thought of that," Doug said. "I mean, after all, you play the guitar all day long your fingers would just be too sore at night."

Before I could probe Doug on just how much fingers figured into the discussion, we were interrupted by the Hostess. "Aren't you going to join the game?" she said.

"Sure," Doug and I both said, even before we knew *what* game.

"We're going to do it differently tonight," the Hostess said. That sounded interesting—to me, anyway, being shut off from the world by two years in the Canadian bush.

"Yes," she continued, "we're going to push each other in the swimming pool but tonight there won't be any water in it."

"Isn't somebody liable to get a skull fracture?" I put forth tentatively.

"Yes, but Dr. Princely is here; he'll be able to handle any situation." I knew Dr. Princely from my previous tenure in Tinselland. He had a perfect medical record. Not one of his patients had ever lived. Dr. Princely performed surgery with all the skill of a trained muskrat skinner. Apocryphal as it may look in cold print, the story still persists that Dr. Princely was actually the surgeon who performed the first heart transplant; unfortunately, his technique, which he had learned from an old Aztec high priest, left much to be desired recovery-wise.

Before we could follow the Hostess to the new game (from which there was no return), the party was blessed by a new and dazzling arrival. Our Italian producer, Frederico Fellucio, who had just completed, Doug Shelby whispered, his sensational new film, *The Rover Boys on the Reeperbahn*, an overground film rated G (or maybe Doug meant "Gee!"). Anyway, Frederico Fellucio was unusual,

which is not an adequate word at all. He had metamorphosed from a rather morose cocoon (at our story conference) into a flaming butterfly. He had enormous rings of
gold and precious stones on each finger and his quota of
fingers seemed more than ordinary mortals. His hair was
long and uncoifed. A hat which must have originally been
worn by Modigliani crushed his eyebrows into craggy
bushes overhanging his black summer-lightning eyes. He
spotted Reiko.

"Ahhhh," Fellucio said, in a language which resembled
English only remotely, "a beautiful Chinese girl!"

"I'm Japanese," Reiko said.

"Ah," Fellucio said, wavering his heavy fingers like
bursting fountains, "I need a beautiful Chinese girl in my
next picture, *The Vestal Virgins of Old Wyoming.* How
do you look nude, my dear?"

"I'm Japanese," Reiko repeated.

One of Fellucio's stooges, who looked like a Sicilian
trigger-man, said, "The Maestro says you are *Chinese!*"
Then he stepped close to Reiko and had a go at looking
evil. I could see an international incident rapidly budding.
"The Maestro is right," I said. "You're Chinese." Reiko
looked at me like I'd suddenly lost my senses, an occur-
rence which had happened long ago.

"The Maestro is never wrong," suggested the Ugly Sicilian.

"How about his last picture?" Doug Shelby said.

"My last picture!" the Maestro screamed, spreading his
bejeweled talons like an eagle over a trapped rabbit. "My
last picture was a masterpiece! All my pictures are master-
pieces!"

"He's right, you know," the Ugly Sicilian said.

"I need a beautiful Chinese girl in my next picture, *The
Vestal Virgins of Old Kentucky,*" Fellucio said to Reiko.
"How do you look nude?"

"How do *you* look nude?" Doug Shelby said.

"Beautiful," the Ugly Sicilian said.

"Not you, him!" Doug Shelby said, indicating the bejeweled Maestro.

"That's who I meant," the Ugly Sicilian said. "He's a beautiful man. A very beautiful man."

"Where? Where?" It was the Hostess again. "Oh, Signor Fellucio, how nice of you to come."

"Of course," Fellucio said, kissing the Hostess' outthrust hands.

"You know everybody, of course," the Hostess said and led the Maestro away toward the fun a little farther away.

"Who's he?" Reiko wanted to know.

"A wop film producer," Doug Shelby said, "who can do no wrong, to hear him tell it. He produces films with stories he makes as he goes along. Also one of his specialties is no titles—just numbers—5½, 5¾, 6⅞. I saw 5½ the other night in Westwood—"

"How was it?" I asked.

"I left at 2¾."

"He's producing the picture Marve and I are writing," I said.

"Are you kidding?" Doug Shelby said. "I'm telling you, he doesn't *use* writers. Who needs writers?"

"Not so loud, you son of a bitch!" Harry Baline said. Harry was a writer who had spent a good twenty years in Hollywood not writing. His recent *pièce de résistance* was a television series starring a lovely black chambermaid, who wore Pucci uniforms and lived in a penthouse high above the Hollywood hills. She also was the mother (according to the plot) of the only uncute black child I have ever seen. This kid was the bore of the ages. The father is never mentioned, presumably because he is on relief and is alive and well and living in Watts where he's heading a sculpture class, which is designed not only to bring culture to Watts but fame and fortune to the chambermaid's husband, which if it does will complicate matters because she has more goddamn suitors than she knows what to do with now. The series is a smash. The only tragic thing about it is that it has reestablished Harry's faith in himself. He's completely dumped the Virgin Mary.

The party was starting to "swing" by this time. This is a word I have picked up from an old Sheilah Graham memoir. The guests were arriving in ever-increasing numbers and styles. Most of the older men dressed like younger men and the younger men dressed like a combination of Lord Douglas and Oscar Wilde and Rosalind Russell. Rosalind Russell arrived dressed as if she expected to be presented at court—on a hit-and-run driving charge. I wish I knew what this meant, but ever since Miss Russell turned down one of my plays for one of Eugene O'Neill's, I have been undermining her. Miss Russell was with her agent, her husband, and a flamingo. Or maybe the flamingo was her agent. It was confusing. They were *all* dressed in pink.

An extremely imperious little man arrived, and judging by his attitude, in other times he would have been at least a Caesar. I've never seen such arrogance and calculated insolence. He blessed everyone within range with a papist aspergillum containing mace. Here, I thought, was a lifetime project for the Dale Carnegie Institute. Immediately when he entered the room, he grabbed every woman he could reach by the inside of her upper thigh. And not one of them noticed.

"I may start drinking heavily again," I said, "just like I used to when I lived in Hollywood before."

"Don't do that," advised Doug, "stick to dope."

"You're sweet," I said.

"Let's move up closer to the bar," Doug said. "Maybe I'll be able to pick up some information about something I can make some money with. You never can tell with these bastards—they're liable to let something slip."

We passed the famous Frederico Fellucio on our way. He was on his hands and knees, barking like a dog and lifting his leg on a potted palm. I heard someone whisper, "I don't care *what* he won at Cannes—I still think he should be house-broken. A good whack on the ass with a rolled-up newspaper—that's the way to do it."

"Who's that?" Reiko said, indicating Fellucio.

"Lassie," Doug Shelby said.

"I don't understand," Reiko said.

"Nobody does," Doug said. "She's not supposed to raise her leg—she's supposed to squat."

The bar was eight-people deep. All shouting the funniest

things to each other. Not a soul was listening. The bartenders were all black and wore their hair Afro-style. They didn't look happy and I was sure they had spears and blowguns ready for a midnight massacre. I resolved to get the hell away from Mrs. Custer's big blow at 11:45 sharp. Not that I mind massacres, but that little alarm clock goes off mighty early on a Monday morning.

As we lingered at the bar, hopefully waiting for our number to be called so we could have a drink, we could hear wild shrieks of merriment coming from the direction of the swimming pool. These wild shrieks of merriment were followed by low moans of agony. I guess Mrs. Custer was telling it true. There *was* no water in the pool. What a lovely party!

"Well, if it isn't the big writer from New York!" It was Johnny Blackwell accompanied by that hail-fellow-well-met, Marty Goodfellow, the New York Bar Association's contribution to the arts. Marty was pleasantly mulled, which meant his sneer was sort of halfway between a snarl and a smirk. He was dressed half Italian and half Shirley Temple. Anything that could be ruffled was. His wrists (both of them) carried matching Vacheron and Constantin wristwatches. His face flared by scotch brightened as he thought up a smart line for me, "Waddya hear from Walden Pond?"

"They got big trouble up there," I said. "Thoreau just killed his agent."

"What's that mean?" Marty Goodfellow stiffened right up tight. He figured that he might have been insulted. He hadn't, but I could see it coming in the not-too-distant future.

"Marty, relax!" Johnny Blackwell said. "Right away he wants to start a fight," he explained to me. "Marty is just a little too tense for his own good. One of these days he's gonna drop dead. I just hope it isn't right before the show."

"I'd never do that, Johnny," Marty said. "You know me better than that." Then Marty said to me, "Isn't he a great guy?"

"Who?" I said.

"The boss," Marty said, tensing up again.

"Who's the boss?" Reiko said.

"Jesus H. Christ!" Marty screamed.

"My father won't like *that*," Reiko said. "He's a Buddhist priest."

Marty selected his most vicious expression, flashed it at us, and flung himself toward the bar.

"Nice chap," I said.

"Where?" Johnny said.

At two A.M. the party was still going strong, but we weren't. Life in the bush had not built up my resistance to sleep. I was dead on my feet, but most everybody else just seemed to be getting started. The girls were screaming upon feeling cold fingers whoopsed between their legs, and coarse laughter grew coarser and less well timed.

A couple of heavy-handed cowboy actors had pawed Reiko a bit. She just looked at them and they faded away. One actor, who had been the star of a South Sea island series a few years ago, sent a roving pockmarked emissary over to proposition Reiko. "How would she like to come up to Rory Camfron's apartment?"

"Who's he?" Reiko wanted to know.

"You remember Rory Camfron; he was the star of *Moon over the Southern Sea*. He was the captain of the schooner that used to go around picking up coconuts and girls. Remember?"

"Oh, yes," Reiko said, "I didn't like him."

"How could you not like him?"

"I watched the show every week," Reiko said.

"Then you don't want to come up to his apartment?"

"Why doesn't he ask me himself?" Reiko said.

"He's a star."

"He wasn't a star even when he was a star," said Irving Laveeeene who had just materialized from nowhere. "And why don't you pack up your pockmarks in your old kit bag and get the hell outa here?"

"How would you like a fat lip?" Pockmarks said.

"Are you mad?" Irving said. "You'd *dare* to say a thing like that to a holder of the *black belt?*"

This last remark made things happen very quickly.

First, the black belt holder found himself suddenly lying on the floor, then he found himself being lifted off the floor by his lapels, and Pockmarks said, "Say you're sorry about my face!"

Irving didn't have much left in his lungs but he managed to squeak out a pockmark apology. Pockmarks immediately dropped him, from a considerable height, and left.

"That's the younger generation for you," Irving said. "No goddamn respect for black belt holders. I need a drink." The crowd at the bar had thinned by this hour and Irving had no trouble reaching one of the Zulu bartenders and downing a triple scotch, plus a clip of tranquilizers, which he was never without.

"Let's go home," Reiko said.

"Why?" I said, just to be contrary. "Isn't this what you've been waiting for for two years up in the Canadian wilderness—the bright lights of Hollywood?"

"Yes," Reiko said, "but—it's not much fun."

"You think Canada is fun?"

"No."

"You wanna go back there?"

"Yes."

"But," I said, "you said it was no fun."

"It isn't," Reiko said, her eyes suddenly getting moist.

I gave her my handkerchief. "Then why do you want to go back there?"

"I miss Bennie the Beaver."

I thought she was putting me on, although she never has. "Bennie the Beaver" is a name I have given one of our most persistent animal visitors at Lost Lake. He always arrives about dusk, heaves his huge body (beavers are a lot larger than most people think or care) out of the water, and comes up on the bank to munch some particular kind of growth which we seem to have on our little island.

"I miss Bennie the Beaver, too," I said, "but think of all the money we're making here in Hollywood, the glamor capitol of the world."

"Look at all the money we're spending," Reiko said.

"Everything costs more here."

"I know," I said, "but it's glamorous. You'll never see any movie and television stars walking down the street at Lost Lake."

"The only movie and television star we've seen walking down the street here was Flipper and he wasn't walking—he was swimming."

"That was during the rainy season," I said. "California has two seasons—rainy and smoggy. Sometimes they have both at once and it's a very good thing."

"Why?" Reiko said.

"Because everybody dies," I said, feeling myself getting in too deep.

"Even at Palm Springs?" Reiko was warming up to this whole thing.

"Nobody dies in Palm Springs," Irving said, beaming up to us, bright with alcohol.

"If nobody dies," Reiko said, "what happens to them?"

"Let me put it another way," Irving said. "If someone does die in Palm Springs, no one ever notices it."

I started to get very interested in this. "What do you mean?"

"Well," Irving said, "if nobody ever gets out of his golf cart, how can you tell?"

This made sense.

12

MARVE and I didn't have the story line of *The Devil and the Hot Virgin* whipped, but we were sure beating the hell out of it. The conception of Johnny Blackwell as a monk in the Great St. Bernard Pass, high up in the Alps, didn't seem to work out. It is very difficult to be funny wearing a shaved head and a cassock, and we also reasoned that Johnny as a sometimes-eccentric dancer, might want to throw in a few eccentric dance steps, which could be done, deep inside the voluminous folds of his cassock, but the audience would never know what he was doing unless he lifted his monkish robes like a cancan dancer, which might be awkward. Then for a little while we had him as Scottish monk dressed in a mini-kilt, but on second thought and a long conversation with Bishop Sheen—or was it Al Capp? Maybe it was Yvonne De Carlo—anyway, we abandoned this idea, too. Gradually we found ourselves drifting back to the original story of *The Devil and the Hot Virgin*. We weren't copping out. We were being practical. What was the point of trying to think of a new story when the old story was just as lousy?

After five days of intensive, backbreaking, bloodsweating labor, Marve and I came up with something we hoped would satisfy the undeveloped comedic insight of Marty Goodfellow and the meat and potatoes attitude of Johnny Blackwell's comedy style, plus something which Frederico Fellucio might not understand:

The Devil and the Hot Virgin

The scene: *Dawn in the Amazon jungles (of South*

104

*America). Long shot of Mount Goo-boo,
rising above the mists of the valleys far below. Suddenly a terrifying rumble is
heard—Mount Goo-boo, a volcano, suddenly erupts spewing white-hot lava ten
miles into the air—cut to* TAB HOOPER
*(Johnny Blackwell) a Peace Corps worker
peacefully asleep in a grapevine hammock
with three luscious Amazon maidens. At the
sound of exploding Mount Goo-boo:*

TAB:
(springing from his hammock):
What—was that?
1ST AMAZON MAIDEN:
That Mount Goo-boo. He Devil. You like Tondelayo?
TAB:
(taking her into his arms):
Of course I like you, Tondelayo. You're so warm and
soft and—
2ND AMAZON MAIDEN:
You like Taratara?
TAB:
(taking 2nd Amazon maiden into his arms):
Of course I like you, Taratara. You're so warm and soft
and—
3RD AMAZON MAIDEN:
You like Tongabonga?
TAB:
(taking 3rd Amazon maiden into his arms):
Of course I like you, Tongabonga. You're so warm and
soft and—

(A WITCH DOCTOR *enters. He wears a frighten-
ing mask and carries a long pole with a human
skull on top of it.)*

WITCH DOCTOR:
You like Witch Doctor?

TAB:

I *admire* you.

WITCH DOCTOR:

Devil mountain angry—make big boom boom— want'um virgin.

TAB:

Gee, the Peace Corps never told us about situations like this, but I don't think we can hand over a virgin whenever the Devil mountain is in the mood. I don't think Senator Fulbright would approve. I don't think he would approve at all.

WITCH DOCTOR:

Old Amazon custom. For five thousand years, every day Devil mountain want virgin for sacrifice.

TAB:

Just *sacrifice?* That's all?

WITCH DOCTOR:

It's usually enough.

TAB:

What would happen if you don't give Devil mountain what it wants?

WITCH DOCTOR:

(*rattling his skull on pole and beating his tom-toms*): Devil mountain destroy village.

TAB:

That's all? It's not much of a village, you know.

WITCH DOCTOR:

Peace Corps white man from United States speak with forked tongue.

TAB:

I know. It's one of the older courses they have at Berlitz —goes back to the days when it was part of the Indianization of the Indian.

1ST AMAZON MAIDEN:

You like Tondelayo?

WITCH DOCTOR:

Sure I like Tondelayo. I also like Taratara and Tongabonga. (*The three Amazon maidens giggle.*)

(Off in the distance we hear an ever-increasing roar coming from Mount Goo-boo—it grows angrier.)

TAB:
This isn't at all like Texas.

WITCH DOCTOR:
Come now. Must make sacrifice of virgin to Devil mountain or village will be destroyed.

(The WITCH DOCTOR makes an attempt to drag one of the girls out the door of the tiny hut. They all scream hysterically.)

TAB:
Doctor, you can't do this. You can't carry into perpetuity this silly myth of the Devil mountain who must be satisfied with a virgin every day.

WITCH DOCTOR:
Listen, White Boy, I been a witch doctor here for almost fifty years—I'll decide what's good for the town and what ain't!

(The WITCH DOCTOR grabs TONDELAYO and drags her screaming through the front door and up toward the Devil mountain.)

CUT TO: *Goo-boo, the Devil mountain—the old WITCH DOCTOR picks up TONDELAYO and flings her into the boiling lava. Immediately the lava stops boiling and all is quiet.*

CUT TO: *TAB HOOPER kneeling in prayer in front of a small makeshift altar.*

TAB:
And bless Mommy and Daddy, and help me keep up the good work here in the jungles of the Amazon. Amen.

(The two Amazon maidens who are left, TARATARA and TONGABONGA, are giggling in the background.)

TAB:

(*his eyes heavenward*):

Why do they always laugh? What's so funny about being an Episcopalian?

TARATARA:

(*snuggling up to him*):

You like Taratara?

TAB:

Yeah, makes my job down here a lot easier.

TONGABONGA:

You like Tongabonga?

TAB:

Yeah, makes my job down here a lot easier.

(*Both Amazon maidens giggle again.*)

TARATARA:

You got wife back in the States?

TAB:

Yes, as a matter of fact she's joining me here this afternoon to help me with my work.

TONGABONGA:

Your wife come here we have her thrown into volcano. I go tell Witch Doctor.

TAB:

Now wait a minute, girls. We've been married for quite some time now, Myrna and I, and I don't think she is what the volcano has on order.

TARATARA:

What does that mean?

TAB:

Well, to put it bluntly, my wife is not a virgin.

TONGABONGA:

That's all right. What does a volcano know? I go tell Witch Doctor.

TAB:

(*nervously*):

Please, Tongabonga, wait. Let's talk this thing over.

(*At this moment we again hear the rumblings*

and movements of the Devil mountain—but louder and more terrifying this time.)

TAB:

Not again! *Two* virgins in one day??? Why?

TARATARA:

Inflation come to Amazon jungles, too.

TAB:

But I came down here to avoid all that!

(*At that moment a handsome young man enters. He is dressed in a small sheepskin and has cloven hoofs and horns. The two Amazon maidens scream and run from the hut.*)

TAB:

(*to the new arrival*):

My name is Tab Hooper. I'm with the Peace Corps.

THE DEVIL (*of the mountain*):

I know.

TAB:

You know?

THE DEVIL:

Yes, the Devil is everywhere and knows everything.

TAB:

You're not—the devil—from the mountain?

THE DEVIL:

Oh, yes. I came down to check up and see how many virgins they got left. I may have to move to another mountain, closer to a larger town. That is, if the virgin supply is getting low.

TAB:

(*relieved*):

That's a good idea. If you want, I'll help you pack. There are no more virgins around here.

THE DEVIL:

What about Taratara and Tongabonga?

TAB:

Taratara and Tongabonga? Oh, yes. Well, they left. I

sent them to visit my mother in Beeville—that's a little town in Texas.

THE DEVIL:

(*vituperously*):

You lie! Yankee dog!

TAB:

(*spunkily*):

Now, you just wait a minute there, Mr. Devil!

THE DEVIL:

Tell you what I'm gonna do. You sell your soul to me
and I won't have Taratara and Tongabonga thrown
into the volcano to try and satisfy my insatiable taste
for virgins. How's that for a deal?

"How's that for a script," Marve said to Johnny Blackwell, Marty Goodfellow, Frederico Fellucio and Miss
Zooker.

"It's a piece of shit!" Johnny said.

"It's a piece of shit!" Marty said.

"It's a piece of shit!" Fellucio said—then there was a
pause.

"Miss Zooker—?" questioned Marve.

"It's a piece of shit!" Miss Zooker said.

Never in my entire writing career have I witnessed such
a solid front of unanimous agreement. Marty slitted his
eyes and hardened his tone and said to Marve, "What do
you and Jack think of it?"

"We think it's a piece of shit," Marve said modestly.

13

BACK in the wilderness, I always seemed to be busy and there were never enough hours in any day to do what I wanted to do. But here in the Golden West, I was finding time on my hands. This could have been because I was missing more and more Johnny Blackwell meetings, because there were more and more of them, and they accomplished less and less. Johnny Blackwell, who would have been a number one lush if he tried just a little bit harder, showed up more or less mulled every time Marty Goodfellow, who seemed to have a little more power lately, called for a meeting.

Most of the time I didn't know about these jolly get-togethers because I stopped answering my telephone after 11 A.M. Marty Goodfellow, who regularly cheated on his wife, usually arrived home between two and three in the morning and immediately got on the horn to shake things around a bit in the writers' bullpen. I don't know what the other writers did to discourage these just-before-dawn messages from this jovial Garcia (he was always jovial after knocking off some innocent hooker), but a phone which doesn't answer is a surefire method. Marty would always say, when he managed to corner me, which wasn't often anymore, "I called you last night. Where the hell were you?"

"Last night?" I'd say. "Oh, yes—last night we were at a PTA meeting."

"Until three o'clock in the morning?" he'd say.

"Yes," I'd say. "The principal of Bobby's school can't get there till two—he moonlights until two—he's the Avon lady for Laurel Canyon." (EDITOR'S NOTE: Laurel Canyon

111

is a district in the Hollywood Hills populated by brownies, pixies and elves, and Peter the Hermit's children, a boy named Sue and a girl named George Patton.)

The time I accumulated from not having to listen to Johnny Blackwell slob his way through an excruciatingly funny routine, while Marty kept up his forced laughter for hours on end with the other unfortunates at the conference table in various states of catatonia, I put to good use. I spent most of the time taking stock not of my life but of my mountains and molehills of carefully typewritten notes, which I have accumulated over a period of hundreds of years (from the look of the mountains).

Actually, by burrowing my way into and around this mass of trivia, I was doing the job I was paid every week to do. I was hoping I might find some material or a routine or two which might be used in *The Devil and the Hot Virgin* if the movie ever got to a sound stage.

During my days of careful research, which more resembled a finicky trash man trying to arrange neatly his collection of wastepaper as to size, shape and texture, I didn't find too much which would help Johnny Blackwell become the world's greatest movie star because my notes were too random, too unrelated and too esoteric, even for me, the father of this mighty pile. The meanings of most of it eluded me completely:

"Impeach Jane Fonda." This is just a line which I had apparently thought would make a nice bumper sticker, and also it is something I will probably never do anything about (so far as bumper stickers are concerned). Jane Fonda has always fascinated me. This girl, who looks so much like her father, has had to spend most of her adult life taking off her clothes to prove that she's not Henry.

"Do THREE things each day—that's all." This note has been taken care of. It is obviously a rule of life. Daily life. Well, I *do* do three things a day. I get up in the morning. I eat. I go to bed at night. Anything else I do is pure gravy. No wonder I have very few gray hairs. My conscience is absolutely clear.

"Katherine Hepburn now sounds like George Arliss in *Disraeli*—looks like him, too." This item I put down after seeing the Tony Awards on television. Katherine did or did not win an award, I don't remember. All I remember is that this once lovely, ethereal creature of the movies had changed so much as to be almost unrecognizable. Oh, *why* don't they *quit?* Why do they always have to come back and spoil everything? *I'm* not getting any older—why should *they????*

Lassie and *Wild Kingdom.* These two are, of course, television shows. Lassie almost always is the savior of the wild creatures of the forest who are in trouble. She even saves people sometimes, which is her only weakness. On one particular show in the spring of 1970, a young deer was presumably run almost to death by two punks on snowmobiles. To get the effect of complete exhaustion and also to handle the young deer, it had to be doped supposedly by a tranquilizer. This is all very well, but in the case of deer—and also with lots of other wild animals—these tranquilizers, more often than not, cause death. Watching this episode of *Lassie,* I wondered how many deer had died to make this show.

The *Wild Kingdom* show, narrated and acted in by Marlin Perkins of the St. Louis Zoo. Mr. Perkins may be a helluva zoo keeper, but his speech coach must have been Ronald the Robot. *Wild Kingdom* is the same each week, but with different animals. Although bull and bear fights have been prohibited over most of the world for generations now, *Wild Kingdom* has brought back a version of this cruel sport. Wild animals, evidently photographed in some sort of woodland pit, from which they cannot escape, are thrown together and are shown alternately biting and clawing at each other. Then supposedly separating and going on their way, none the worse for wear—they'd like to make you think. But when you put a beaver up against a cougar, somebody's going to get hurt, and so far no bets have been placed on the beaver.

This goes on week after week. I just wonder how many beavers they lose for each sequence. Or how many cougars (in a free-for-all with a grizzly). Or how many woodchucks during a carefully staged pier-six brawl with a badger. The ASPCA seems to have been particularly lax in their supervision of this series. Or maybe the whole thing is photographed abroad and out of its jurisdiction.

If anyone feels I am making too much of this, so be it.

The next item in my ton of notes is: "Check passport—go back to Tahiti." This of course is dream stuff. I will probably never get a chance to go back to Tahiti, which is sad. Some of the loveliest moments in my life were spent sipping the delectable Tahitian coffee, just as the sun was rising over the mountains in back of me. The first streaks of pink and gold lighting the long line of crashing surf, beating itself into froth on the reef which protects the harbor at Papeete. No one ever seemed to be up at this hour except me and the pretty Chinese-Tahitian waitress who kept my coffee cup filled.

The days were always soft and cool in Tahiti, no matter what the temperature was. This is the way it seemed to me—while the nights were soft under billions of stars and always with the sensuous beat of the Tahitian drums somewhere off in the distance. Neither Captain Cook's crew nor Marlon Brando's completely spoiled this place, and I still love it, which is strange for a man with a similar passion for ice and snow and the cold arctic wastes. I still have a paradoxical yearning for the South Pacific (in spite of the movie). Maybe Charlie Manson is right. Maybe I *am* quaint.

"Make a list of the big shots I know." This is another note in my endless file. I don't know exactly, or I don't remember, why I put this down. Was it because I had blackmail in mind, or because of my ego, or because I needed a loan, or because of all three? I'll never know, and I never made the list, but it has set me to thinking, as my grandfather used to say when he glimpsed my grandmother in the nude.

I've known quite a few big shots, but, unlike Sammy in B. Schulberg's long-ago novel, I haven't taken advantage of this, which is silly because we all know it isn't *what*, it's *who* you know. Right, Lord Snowden?

"Dial a Prayer," one of my notes, is a telephone service provided by someone (I don't know who). I made a note of it because I think it is a wonderful idea. For instance, you aren't feeling well—you call your doctor—he isn't available—you're all out of aspirin anyway, so what do you do? You dial a prayer, and a voice which sounds like Fredric March's comes on and intones, "Now I lay me down to sleep. I pray the Lord my soul to keep. If I should die before I wake. . . ." This last may shake you up a little, especially if you're not too sure of the immediate future as it is. And you're all out of aspirin.

There are lots of services you can dial nowadays. If you're a drunk, you have a choice. You can dial someone to come over and keep you from drinking or someone who will drink *with* you (if he doesn't drive off a cliff on the way over). If you have a dope problem and need help, you can dial a pusher. Or if you're a pusher and business is slack, you can dial for a mailing list.

You can dial ten minutes of Hugh Hefner's philosophy, which may help you get through the night or give you that extra little something you need to slash your wrists.

You can dial another ten minutes of the Japanese philosophy of John Lennon, as taught by Yoko Ono. The first nine minutes of this particular service is consumed by John Lennon's description of Yoko's posterior, which if you've seen those album covers is not nearly enough time.

Another note: "Idea for title of magazine article on river sewage pollution, 'Are We Shitting Ourselves to Oblivion?' " I sent this idea in sketch form with the title to several magazines, but so far I haven't heard from any of them. I thought surely I'd hear from my dear friend, Jack Mack Carter, the editor of the *Ladies' Home Journal*, but maybe he reasons that a "lady" would not be interested in tracing an effluvial voyage to its final destination. He could be right—a turd is not the *Kon-Tiki*.

My notes, as I said, are endless. And with my inability to stop making them, I feel I have at least approached within easy reach perpetual motion. I will spare you and myself the chore of wading through them (at this time anyway). The last note, which I will touch on here, concerns Stanmar, a house prefabricating concern in Boston. My experience with them in Connecticut is probably the experience of many in these days of housing shortages. For two dollars, Stanmar will send you a booklet full of prefab houses they sell—to be erected on your lot within something like three or four weeks—and that's about it. You pays your two dollars and you gets your booklet and you orders your prefab house—and there the whole operation *ceases*. You never hear from Stanmar again. No one ever calls. No one ever answers your letters. It's as if they never existed. But they do, and I've finally decided what they are doing. They are not selling *prefab houses* to be erected on your lot; they are selling *booklets*—for two dollars.

We waited three weeks, at that time, for some action because we were desperate for a house, but nothing ever happened. A friend suggested I get off a letter to them, running something like this: "There's no such thing as a two-dollar whore anymore. Why don't *you* raise *your* price?"

14

HACKETTSVILLE, California, is a long way from Hollywood, California, and even farther (to me) from our home at Lost Lake, but Reiko, who turned out to be less like a helpless dependent and uncertain little Lotus Blossom and more like an inosculation of Genghis Khan, Attila the Hun, and Napoleon Bonaparte, decided that Bobby should continue to go to a regular school with regular children instead of having to be uncertainly tutored by me in a lonely log cabin, far from any possibility of softball at recess time.

I had long ago gotten pretty fed up with second- and third-grade math, spelling, and finger-painting, but I *was* looking forward to teaching Bobby fourth-grade geography. The fourth-grade geography books had pictures of New Guinea broads with bare knockers. I had anticipated with what almost amounted to enthusiasm the education of a nine-year-boy in this direction. The geography of the human female, even in its most primitive form, was very important to a boy's overall understanding of what he was going to be up against in the years to come. I didn't want Bobby to wind up on his wedding night screaming "wow!" It might inhibit his bride and confuse his intentions.

This is why we stayed in California. So our kid could be like everybody else's kid. That's the American way.

Hackettsville, California, is about as far away from Hollywood as one could get and still be within a more or less convenient commuting distance, which with the precarious status of *The Devil and the Hot Virgin* was not too bad an idea. I expected to be called back at any moment and do it over again—maybe this time as a musical.

And I was contractually bound to any insane whim of my employers. I felt like an indentured servant, which is what movie writers, in fact, are.

I had remembered Hackettsville from my meanderings in the days when I called California home. It was a very small community, as yet undiscovered, in the lovely Peach Valley, surrounded by the foothills of the Tehachapi Mountains.

We bought a lovely 50-acre "ranch" nestled in the arms of a cozy little canyon.

The land was thick with large groves of pine, hemlock, white and black birch, live oak and many other varieties of growth, with which I was unfamiliar and didn't intend to bone up on. As an early-day movie producer once said, "A tree is a tree," which is probably the last sensible statement ever made in Hollywood.

Our newly acquired home was a small yellow house which came from Sears in sections and was bolted together so it would be more or less continuous. After the great openness of our Canadian home and the mansionlike mausoleum we lived in in Roxbury Hills, the Hackettsville hacienda seemed very confining and inconvenient. Most of our worldly goods, including my six-ton library, were stored in a huge barn, which was also part of this spread. We would have been better off living in the barn, but there was the problem of heat and plumbing. The problem was—there wasn't any.

We also had another problem the very first day we moved in. The well suddenly went dry. Or so I thought. As usual, instead of keeping a cool head so I could think, I immediately became enraged and called a local moving van company. The local company sent over four medium-sized trucks the same afternoon—an unheard of phenomenon, which I attributed to the splendidly explosive and impassioned display of my histrionic ability in this time of imagined stress. That's all it was—my great ability to make a super tragedy out of any minor incident cost us more than a thousand dollars to remove all of our household goods to the trucking company's warehouse and then in turn move it all back again to our little yellow house.

The well hadn't run dry at all. A fuse had blown causing the pump to malfunction. A thousand hard-earned dollars right down the toilet (at least the toilet worked) just because I had panicked.

Reiko was an angel all through this, and she has never let me forget for an instant that she was an angel all through this. I think she saw through my subtle scheme to get the hell out of Hackettsville and back to the Canadian bush, where I felt I belonged. She had been against the Hackettsville location from the first because she thought it was too far from everything. It was the story of Lost Lake all over again, only this time it didn't make any sense at all. We were five minutes from Hackettsville itself—a metropolis of one grocery store, one liquor store, one post office and a place that sold hammocks made in Mexico. Does this sound like we were too far from everything? I think not.

Getting Bobby to school from this new (civilized) location wasn't quite as difficult as it was from Lost Lake, with its 13-mile snowmobile ride through the woods to the school bus stop, but it wasn't as convenient as it might have been. I had to drive him about a mile to where Mrs. Sutfin picked him up in her station wagon (which was called a feeder bus) which drove him to a rendezvous with the real school bus, which carried him to the Alamo Creek grammar school. This was a fairly fast trip because Mrs. Sutfin was the Stirling Moss of the foothills of the Tehachapis. She didn't know the meaning of the word "fear." The kids' hair turned white overnight, but she didn't know the meaning of the word "fear." I used to say a short prayer which got longer and longer every time I saw her burn rubber on takeoff.

The townspeople of Hackettsville were warm, helpful, and very friendly. Apparently no one had told them they were out of step with the rest of the world. This didn't mean that they were stupid. Far from it. From the most humble small farmer to the sophisticated writers, artists, and artisans who lived in this area, they were all the same. Maybe it was all the fault of the serenity of the surrounding peaceful country. It was easy to imagine an Indian silently paddling his birch canoe along the mostly placid waters of the lovely Tejon River in the early morning mists. Or to imagine a proudly aloof white-tailed buck lowering his magnificently antlered head to drink his fill in the cool of the evening.

The Indians didn't silently paddle along the Tejon anymore, but once in a while you could see a white-tailed buck. How these lovely animals, who lived almost side by side with the red savage, managed to still live in the same way with the white savage may be nature's way of warning us of what's in store for the conquerors of the earth. This super race which is now in charge. "Leave us not forget," as my old anthropology professor used to say: "The dinosaurs all died, but the possums lived on."

But enough of prophecy. "The world of tomorrow was yesterday." That's something else my old anthropology professor used to say. Maybe I should mention my old anthropology professor was relieved of his professorship after they caught him molesting a female gorilla. The authorities would have forgiven him and the whole thing would have been hushed up, but he insisted he wanted to marry her. That kind of thing was frowned on in those days BKB (Before Kingman Brewster).

I was as happy as I could be in Hackettsville, or, I should say, I was as I could be 2,000 miles southwest of where I felt I should be. Reiko soon began to love Hackettsville and its proximity to people with whom she never bothered to mingle. Funny—and human, too, I suppose. Most people are terrified at the thought of not being within shouting distance of neighbors whom they have no interest in and who in an emergency would usually be of no help. I mean of no *real* help. They're not doctors, or nurses, or even sober in time of trouble. But they're *there!*

Reiko has often said, "I like to see lights at night. Look down there in the valley—see the lights." This was comforting to her. To me it meant one thing: unhappy souls who couldn't sleep, or happy souls watching Griffin, Cavett, or Carson, or Ronald Coleman and Irene Rich and May McAvoy starring in *Lady Windermere's Fan*—costarring Bert Lytell. (If you haven't seen this movie, stay up sometime. It's always on the 3:00 A.M. *Matinee Theatre*.)

No matter what the song says, people who need people are not the luckiest people in the world. They're just scared.

The people in Hackettsville didn't need people too much, which I thought was a great part of its charm. They had their church suppers, their fireman's balls, and their cultural centers, where they could gather almost every Saturday night and listen to the Ray Charles Dancers, or watch the June Taylor Singers. Then afterward have coffee and strudel. There was no wife-swapping in Hackettsville, principally because after an evening of culture they were too inspired, and, besides, some of the wives couldn't be swapped for a lame horse.

Our little yellow house began to inspire *us* to new heights in friendly hostility. Reiko and I had always been like two alley cats who loved each other madly but couldn't resist a good fight. At any time. Day or night, we were ready, and the cramped quarters of our little house didn't help us become an overnight Heloise and Abelard, or Jackie and Ari, or Sophia and Carlo.

The house was so narrow we couldn't pass each other without taking a deep breath, and the kitchen was in the living room, which was also my office. The bathroom might just as well have been in the living room, too, because of some acoustical phenomenon: When one pushed the vitreous china lever to flush the toilet, one got five full minutes of the sound of Victoria Falls. The first time we heard this overwhelming sonata stupendza, Reiko and I were sitting in the living room and it was Bobby who triggered this new audio experience. Reiko immediately snatched baby Timothy from his little red fire engine and rushed outside to higher ground. I saved my autographed photo of Jane Keane and joined her.

"What about Bobby?!" Reiko screamed.

"It's too late," I said. "Who could live through that?"

Actually, I'm exaggerating slightly, but the toilet was an ever-present and excellent conversation piece for white-water enthusiasts.

But the bathroom wasn't the main problem. It was just one of many, and my having to peck away at my Model No. 5 1926 Remington in the same room with a screaming baby, a nine-year-old boy who insisted on playing with his Hot Wheels right next to my plywood work table, and the Iron Butterfly muttering, "Goddamn this kid," while she whipped up a delicious dinner of seaweed-wrapped rice (which I, strange as it seems—or does it?—liked very much). Reiko's "Goddamn this kid" never indicated which kid, which I thought was an example of splendid impartiality. Or maybe it was just her inability to sort out the English language. Above the babel of mother, children, and crashing dishes, the television set was turned up about as high as it could get without taking off through the ceiling. Bobby had to have it on even through no one was watching it. The sound of the reruns of 1957 *I Love Lucy* shows filled every inch of our little yellow house like a blast of nerve gas.

The whole thing finally got to be too much. We decided to build a new house. This is like a man quitting his job as a certified public accountant to take up a career of fire walking. Or joining the Ku Klux Klan in downtown Newark. Or wearing feathers at a turkey shoot. It was the wrong time to have anything to do with anybody in the building trade, but we were desperate, and as George Eliot said, "What we call desperation is often only the painful eagerness of unfed hope." Or maybe it was Elliott Gould who said that. Or Yvonne De Carlo.

Anyway, this desperation or unfed hope for more living space needled me into dashing headlong into this extremely unsound, precarious, and wildly campy, I thought, venture. Who else but a Tahitian-born Irish dreamer would attempt to build a house in an economic atmosphere about as stable as a vial of nitroglycerine in the hands of a St. Vitus victim with an alcohol problem. On New Year's Eve.

We first contacted a good friend, from New Canaan, Connecticut, who just happened to be an architect. A very fine architect, but a lousy businessman *then*. He improved considerably in that direction after his experience with me.

Being a somewhat, or, I should say, a *total* failure when it came to making good deals for myself, I maneuvered fairly well (quite inadvertently) with Dan—Dan Kistler, the architect—and he agreed to design us a house at far below his usual fee, and I agreed as part of the deal to let him use my beloved Lost Lake lodge whenever he wanted it.

This was the best arrangement I had ever made. The house Dan designed was fascinatingly unique. It was three stories high with a splendid office for me on the top floor—with a view I knew I'd have to shield my eyes from or I'd spend my days looking at the jagged peaks of the high Sierra which could be seen over the foothills of the Tehachapis. This doesn't sound very much like it would turn anybody on but a writer, who is very much like the prisoner in solitary, who falls in love with a cockroach and marries it, knowing full well that the marriage will never be consummated. Later, much later, when the house and my office were completed, I stared out my large picture windows toward these unattainable mountains, which were 70 miles away to the north, and became infatuated. There wasn't one I would leave my wife and family for, but the idea of having a mountain for a mistress held a strange mystique for me. And it was a lot safer than falling for some topless cocktail waitress who is married to a mugger. Then again, maybe I'd better stick to cockroaches—they're not pretty, but they're faithful.

The day the jolly cement pourers poured the foundation for our new house was a day to try men's souls, or at least the souls of the cement jockeys because it was the day of the big blizzard. The big *November* blizzard. Which was unheard of, except in higher California altitudes, which could have the four seasons all in twenty-four hours. However, the foundation group persevered, and the foundation was poured and we were ready for the carpenters. But not quite ready, as we found out after we got the first week's labor bill (we were contracting this project ourselves) which was considerably different from and higher than the price agreed upon. This was just the beginning. It was *Mr. Blandings Builds His Dream House* all over again, with a

few shocking variations, such as the plastering contractor
who suddenly, halfway through the job, demanded an extra $50 for his trouble. I don't know what his trouble was,
but rather than gun him down then and there and getting
fined $10 for killing a plasterer, we paid him the extra 50.

The man who built the fireplace, which I venture to say
is the largest anywhere west of the Mississippi, and maybe
the world, with the exception of the one at San Simeon,
was and is a genius—but a slow genius. He started the
fireplace after the house was finished and we were living
in it—and he was still working on it—six months later. He
laid eight or ten enormous fieldstones each day, while
playing his portable radio at its loudest pitch and always
tuned in to Merv Griffin's local radio station which plays
nothing but country and Western music, and every few
minutes, between and during Johnny Cash and Bobbie
Gentry and Eddie Arnold, etc., some demented disk
jockey screams out something about Merv Griffin. What?
I don't know, but there's no doubt who owns that station
and the air for miles and miles around.

Adam Bilski, who created our magnificent fireplace with
his two strong hands and a lot of stronger rocks, is also
the owner of a fishing camp on First Connecticut Lake,
which, to make it confusing, is located at the very
northern tip of New Hampshire, and every once in a while
when he isn't cracking stones with his rock hammer and
playing his radio at our place, he's flying to New Hampshire to attend a town meeting. It takes about four days
out of the week, but he hasn't missed a town meeting in
twenty years, he told me.

"What the hell do you talk about at a town meeting?" I
asked him.

"The town," he said, and went back to shaping a
vicious-looking glacier-scarred stone into a friendly fireplace rock.

Reiko informed the motley, by then, group of artisans
that we would be moving into our new home by the 15th
of February. This shook some of the frivolity which had
pervaded these expensive hammer owners, some of whom
could not be classified as carpenters—they were simply, as

they were also known locally, as hammer owners. And after observing some of their more delicate work around windows and other fitted necessaries, I concluded there was a good deal of the vandal in them, too. They could take a $20 sheet of pine plywood and in no time at all make it look like a $2-whorehouse linoleum floor, patronized chiefly by patrons wearing golf shoes.

A couple of them were really good men, but they were demoralized by the jokers they had been given to work with, and also apparently from orders from someone to slow down and make the job last. Not only did this *not* make the job last, but it ended the job right then and there. Very abruptly and definitely, finally. The rest of the work we did ourselves. It was painful and slow, but it was the cheapest labor we had ever used, and most of the time the most efficient. Reiko became the most talked of tile layer in town and I got a number one rating in book-shelves, closets, and cedar fencing.

I lost a few points by sinking our lovely avocado-green sunken bathtub a little more sunken that I had intended. It was my first experience with a quicksand basement.

15

THE Devil and the Hot Virgin was now frantically shooting at the First International 6-Arts Studios. Marve and I were locked in my Roxbury Hills ivory tower, which I still had a lease on, from dawn till dusk trying to keep ahead of the insatiable demands for comedy material. These demands came from Frederico Fellucio, and also from Johnny Blackwell, who had apparently lost his gift of extemporization, Marty Goodfellow, who of course was echoing his client, and the director Gordon Puce, plus other assorted Hollywood geniuses who had been hired to louse up the project.

Marve and I didn't try too hard to please this hungry crowd because we knew it was hopeless, but we did have to show them something by nightfall. Most of the time we spent talking about the good old days in Hollywood, and women. The good old days didn't get equal time with women because to Marve, nothing should get equal time with women, except more women. He was the Mighty Joe Young of roués. He has been in rut twenty-four hours a day of every day, in the twenty or more years that I've known him.

"Don't you get tired?" I asked him.

"Exhausted," he said, smiling contentedly.

One day, after we had split our time between *The Devil and the Hot Virgin* and Marve's affair of the night before, he was standing before the window, purring, when suddenly he said, "Hey, what the hell is that son of a bitch doin' out there?"

I was seated at the typewriter, typing "The quick red

126

fox jumped over the lazy brown dog," so I couldn't get up. "What *is* he doing?" I asked.

"He's sitting up on a lifeguard's stand lookin' for something with a pair of binoculars."

"Oh," I said, "that's my neighbor, John Brothers—he's a lawn nut."

"What the hell is he doing with the binoculars?" Marve said.

"Looking for dandelions," I said.

"He musta seen one," Marve said, "because now he's rushing across the lawn with a flamethrower! Wow! Look at that flame! No dandelion could live through an experience like that."

"That's the idea," I said. "That John Brothers would scorch fifty square miles just to kill one lousy dandelion."

"Gee," Marve said, "*that's* intolerance!"

I remember when I felt the same way about a lawn. Nothing gave me greater pleasure (after a certain age) than a few acres of lush Kentucky blue until I discovered I was sweating harder than a one-armed dairy farmer with a herd of double-uddered Guernseys. I put in so much time as the power behind my power mower and the spreader of Red Star (an enriched product shot from steers) that my typewriter grew cold—ice-cold. It became a mania with me. Friends and family were ruthlessly neglected. My family grew hungry and tattered while I mowed, fertilized, weeded and watered this lovely, thoughtlessly privileged sod. This project took so much time I had to be fed intravenously from a portable barbecue mounted on a golf cart, as I pushed my Toyota fertilizer feeder around and around my sleek, fat lawn, satisfying its every gourmet whim. Our *lawn* was eating better than *we* were. My blue (grass) period ended when we moved up to the wilderness of Lost Lake. There the front lawn was solid rock and berry bushes, which had been there before the Precambrian Era and done very well.

As Marve and I progressed from crisis to crisis with *The Devil and the Hot Virgin* Marve became more and more intrigued with my neighbor, the lawn nut. Whether this was because Marve had lost interest in creating the bomb we were working on for presentation on an ill-prepared and unwarned nationwide television audience, or whether he was really fascinated by John Brothers, the dandelion assassin, I'll never know. I do know that he spent hours staring out of my office window, watching the antics of this unusual man.

Marve's continued surveillance of what was going on next door and my continued false starts and wasted paper were rudely interrupted one smoggy, foggy and dismal day by a wild phone call from the studio.

"Better get your asses down here," Miss Zooker told us, "or the end of the world will be today!"

When Marve and I arrived at the studio, after a record-smashing, terrifying dash through, up, over and around the Hollywood Hills to "The Valley," as it was called, the sound stage was deathly quiet. There wasn't a grip or a stagehand or a cameraman or an assistant in sight. There was just Miss Zooker, now dressed like Isadora Duncan, and wearing space shoes, in keeping with her new position of assistant to the producer, which meant a cut in salary, and at her right sprawled in a chair marked DIRECTOR was the director Roger Wheelock. Opposite him were Marty Goodfellow and Johnny Blackwell in appropriately lettered chairs, plus another individual who didn't look quite human.

"What's new?" Marve said in order to break the silence in a nonbelligerent manner.

Marty was the only one who even looked up. He said, indicating the almost human figure sitting alone on the edge of a camera platform, "That son of a bitchin' Witch Doctor refuses to say a line that you two sons a bitches wrote."

"Which line?" Marve said.

"The line that goes, 'Devil mountain angry—make big boom boom—want 'um virgin.' *That* line."

The Witch Doctor retched.

"See! See!" Marty screamed. "That's what that son of a bitchin' Witch Doctor does every goddamn time we mention that son of a bitchin' line! That son of a bitchin' Witch Doctor is a son of a bitchin' mental case!"

"We can change the line," Marve said.

"No," Marty said, "we paid you guys good money for that line and *by Jesus* we're gonna *use* it!"

Marve and I went over to the Witch Doctor, who hadn't taken off his carved wooden mask.

"Hi," Marve said.

"I belong to the Screen Actors Guild," the Witch Doctor said.

"Good for you," Marve said. "We don't want any scab witch doctors workin' for us. Now what's the problem?"

"I don't wanna say, 'Devil mountain angry—make big boom boom—want 'um virgin.' " He just managed to get it out without being sick. I was almost sick myself.

"How would you like to say it?" Marve asked. This new approach unsettled the actor Witch Doctor for the moment and he couldn't quite make up his mind.

Marve waited, and when the Witch Doctor recovered, he said, "How about if I just said, 'Devil mountain angry. It grows increasingly loud and it won't be satisfied until it has been presented with a lovely young, untried maiden'?" Then he took off his Witch Doctor mask and waited for our decision. He was a pleasant-looking old-young man whom I recognized from many motion pictures, but whose name I never knew.

"Do you think a witch doctor would talk like that?" Marve said. "We're trying to be authentic—like the *National Geographic*."

"Holy Christ!" muttered the Witch Doctor. "Authentic! With a devil mountain making boom boom!"

"Why don't we change it to just one 'boom'?" I said. "Just say, 'Devil mountain angry—make big boom—want 'um virgin.' "

"Yeah," the Witch Doctor said, "that's better. Yeah, I like that—by eliminating the one 'boom' it tightens up the whole sentence." Then he slipped his Witch Doctor mask back on and started shouting, "Devil mountain angry!—make big boom!—want 'um virgin! Devil mountain angry!—make big boom!—Want 'um virgin!—Devil moun-

tain angry!—make big boom!—Want 'um virgin! DEVIL
MOUNTAIN ANGRY MAKE BIG BOOM WANT 'UM
VIRGIN!!!!!!"

Suddenly Marty was on his feet, yelling like a madman,
"Get that son of a bitch out of here before I kill him!"
Then he picked up a long, wicked-looking Amazonian
bush knife and rushed toward the Witch Doctor, who just
managed to open the heavy sound stage door in time and
escape into the studio street. Marty came back, breathing
heavily. He sank down in his chair and closed his eyes.
Marve and I started to leave.

"That's the fourth Witch Doctor we've lost today," Miss
Zooker said, checking his name off her clipboard.

"What'd you expect with dialogue like that?" Marve
said, slamming the sound stage door behind us.

Three hours later the telephone rang and Marve answered it. "Oh?—Okay, if you say so. We aim to
please—" Then he hung up the phone and said, "Marty's
got a new broad he's on the make for."

"How do you know?" I said.

"Because the Witch Doctor is out and a Great White
Goddess is in," Marve said.

16

THE day of liberation finally came. *The Devil and the Hot Virgin* was finished, and everyone agreed we had a winner. This may not be unanimous when the public sees it on their 23-inch (diagonally) blurred color television set. In fact, I had the feeling this was the biggest loser of all time. Between the "superb" ad-libbing of our star and the moronic suggestions of the finagling ferret, Marty Goodfellow, plus suggestions by Sue Ann Morgan, Johnny's costar and current barracuda, what little humor, wit and taste we writers had managed to get secretly into the original script now belonged to the ages. It certainly wasn't in the movie.

Johnny's horny old-lady airline stewardess was in there. This character was his warm blanket and wet thumb of security. No matter what disaster befell the comedic moments in the rest of the movie, he knew the audience would greet his geriatric nympho with warm responsive laughter. This is what *he* believed. I believed something else. I believed that the public was goddamn sick and tired of seeing this sweaty fat man in drag, doing his coffee, tea, or me routine for the ten-thousandth time. But he didn't feel this way. To Johnny Blackwell, this character was sacrosanct—like the Ganges River—or Saint Patrick's Cathedral—or James Arness.

I didn't pray that he was wrong, but I counted on I. A. L. Diamond, the patron saint of motion picture comedy, to take care of him one way or another.

Sue Ann Morgan, a lithe blonde who walked like a cobra, played opposite Johnny as the Devil's secretary in our little Faustian farce. When I first met Sue Ann, she was

131

the prototype of all innocence and corn-fed naïveté. She said she would do anything to get into the movies, and I, in *my* naïveté, had no idea that she meant just that. One weekend in the perfumed hay at Johnny Blackwell's castle had insured her part in the movie and apparently in its sequel—if any.

From this moment on, Sue Ann Morgan metamorphosed from a silly farmyard goose girl to Lucretia Borgia's chemist. During the first day of shooting she was field promoted from private first class to commander in chief. There wasn't anything from camera angles to an extra's eye shadow that she didn't have an opinion on.

"Jesus Christ," Irving Laveeeene muttered, "they hired an ingenue and got Orson Welles."

"She's just nervous and shy," I said, using the standard excuse we all use for bullies, dictators, and Chrysler service department heads.

"Yeah," Irving said, "she's about as nervous and shy as Machine Gun Kelly."

"She must be a great lay," I said, "to acquire this much power in such a short period."

"She's the greatest," Irving said.

"You know?" I said.

"Of course," Irving said. "How do you think she got to meet Marty Goodfellow?"

"What's Marty Goodfellow got to do with it?" I said, my deep-blue eyes open wide.

"Are you for real?" Irving said. "Everything that Johnny Blackwell gets, has to go through Marty. Marty says she puts bells in it."

"What?"

"She puts bells in it," Irving said. "Other broads use a diaphragm. She uses bells—she gets 'em from Hong Kong—they're like those round sleigh bells—only smaller, I guess."

"I've never heard of anything like that before," I said.

"Yeah," Irving said, "every time she gets in the sack it sounds like Santa Claus is comin' to town."

I thought Irving was having another pipe dream until one day, a couple of months later, he sent me a catalog

from a Hong Kong sex store (which has been recently
taken over by Sears), and, sure enough, they were selling
little sleigh bells for sex. They were also pushing something called The Magic Wand of Fu Manchu which could
be worn by the male. This device was much more spectac-
ular. It had a built-in siren and colored lights, and when
this ingenious stimulator was used in conjunction with the
female sleigh bells, it made the whole affair, according to
the catalog copy, New Year's Eve at the Tivoli Gardens.

Sue Ann Morgan wasn't our only problem. Marty
Goodfellow had hired another of his clients, Gordon Puce,
a director, who was part Lassie and part Maria Callas.
His chief directorial qualification seemed to take only one
form. Whenever things went wrong, he stamped his dainty
foot and screamed "What are you *doing* to me?????" What
they were doing to him was obvious after a few days—
they were getting rid of him. Gordon Puce was replaced
by a director who looked like John Huston. He wore a
cap and rough tweeds, and had a face that resembled part
of the six-day bike racetrack. His name was Roger
Wheelock, and I never heard him say a word of any mod-
ern-day language in the remaining six weeks the picture
was being made. So far as anyone knew, he spoke only
early Cro-Magnon. Whenever he gave a direction at the
beginning of a new scene, he would stand up and mumble
three or four sentences of multiple grunts, then look
around to see if he was understood—not that it mattered.
He didn't repeat himself. He just retired to his four-posi-
tion director's chair and took a long slug of something
from his cartridge belt of thermos bottles. Then he would
nod to his assistant who would yell, "Start cranking!" and
the scene would be under way.

I complained about Roger Wheelock to Marty Goodfellow, because although I knew the picture was going to be
a bomb, I felt it would be less so if we had a human director. Marty whispered something about letting well
enough alone, which I found out later meant that Marty
was getting 50 percent of Roger Wheelock's salary. This,
of course, is typical of managers like Marty Goodfellow—they get their cut from anything and everything con-

nected with their clients. If Johnny Blackwell wanted a new car, a summer wardrobe or a cottage at Lake Tahoe, Marty Goodfellow would get him anything he wanted, wholesale—which meant Johnny Blackwell would only have to pay about half again what any peasant from Spokane or Wichita Falls could get it for.

And so the picture forged ahead, like an outgoing garbage scow against an incoming tide. It was slow progress, but day by day we got closer and closer to the dumping grounds.

The last day of shooting was like the first. Nothing. Roger Wheelock, the director, no longer lived the pretense of sipping chicken soup from those thermos bottles; every morning he lined up a battery of brandy bottles, and by the end of the day he had pretty well whipped the overproduction of the cognac people.

The actors, besides the iron butterfly Sue Ann Morgan, were running the show. Johnny Blackwell, who had taken to helping the director deplete his stock, didn't seem to care what was happening. Marty Goodfellow didn't fieldmarshal anymore, and absented himself from the studio as much as he dared, and still remained close enough to kiss Johnny Blackwell's ass when the need arose.

The story of *The Devil and the Hot Virgin* had been changed somewhat. Gone were the Peace Corps worker, the Great White Goddess, the horny volcano and the thousands of virgins and the jungles of the Amazon. In its place we had, as Marty put it, a more down-to-earth, folksy type of story—one that would be understood and loved by everybody and the last shot in the movie was a nude bathtub scene, with two men and a girl, featuring Sue Ann Morgan, who not only did not demand that they work on a closed set (with no spectators or visitors) but she insisted that the studio tours be routed through Stage 8 where we were shooting, and invited to sit in the bleachers, which had been hastily erected the night before, and watch.

The bathtub was larger than life-size because it had to accommodate Johnny, Sue Ann and Lee Morton, who was playing the Devil. Sue Ann, who was supposed to be trying to release Johnny from the clutches of the Devil, to whom Johnny had sold his soul in exchange for the Devil's services in converting Johnny from a simple Puerto Rican dishwasher at Toots Shor's into Joe Namath. As the scene started, the three nudes, Sue Ann, Johnny and the Devil, were in the large tub together. As written in the script, Sue Ann was supposed to cling to Johnny and plead with the Devil to release him from his bargain, but Sue Ann had other ideas. She didn't cling to Johnny; she reached down under the water and grabbed him, then she snaked the long red-painted fingers of her other hand down into the water and grabbed the Devil, saying at the same time, "If you don't release Johnny from his contract, I'll pull your balls off!"

With this the Devil screamed and jumped out of the tub and started to run from the set. Sue Ann didn't let go of the Devil *or* Johnny which created a tableau never to be forgotten by the visiting tourists—especially by a Miss Mabelle Thompson, fifty-four, spinster, 353 Shady Lane, Bemidji, Minnesota. She enjoyed a fatal orgasm.

17

ONE day, when taking care of three juveniles (Bobby, Timothy and me) became a little too much for her, Reiko decided to bring her sister over from Japan to help out. This, like Tojo's Victory Dinner, looked great on paper, but in actual practice it was something else.

When Mitsue Hashimoto arrived at Los Angeles International Airport, I had expected to meet a tiny little geisha-type girl who would peek at me over the edge of her silken fan and say, "You got Hershey bar?" or some other Yankee-inspired pleasantry, but instead a very dignified Japanese gentleman, who looked like he'd just come back from signing the treaty aboard the USS *Missouri*, approached me with a half bow and said, "Are you Mr. Douglas?"

"That depends," I said. "What's your problem?" I had to use this sort of wary acknowledgment because process servers come in many guises.

"I represent Japan Air Lines," he said. "My card."

He gave me a card printed in Japanese. I said, "How do I know you are what it says you are on this card?"

"You don't," he said, "unless you can read Japanese."

"What about Pearl Harbor?" I asked, trying to pick a subject less controversial.

"Japan Air Lines had nothing to do with that," he said, somewhat sharply, I thought.

"Oh?" I said. "Who was it—Aer Lingus?"

"Ah so," he said, "them Irish bastards are apt to do anything. Are you Mr. Douglas?"

I said, "Yes, and I'm an Irish bastard."

136

"Ah so," he said. "Faith and begorra! I have your sister-in-law here."

"Where? In that?" I said, indicating his attaché case, suddenly taken with the thought that maybe Mitsue Hashimoto came as a kit and we would have to put her together before we could take her through customs.

"Not ah so," he said. "She is over there in the VIP waiting room. Stay please. I go get her."

With this *he* bowed and *I* bowed and a very black Skycap started looking on the floor for what we'd dropped. As the Japanese gentleman left, I said to the Skycap, "It's all right, George."

"How'd you know my name?" the Skycap said.

"Because I remember when you were on the Santa Fe *Super Chief*," I said.

"Yeah!" he said. "Those were the days—Pola Negri, Agnes Ayres, Carmel Myers and Big Boy Williams on almost every trip!"

"Those were the days," I agreed.

"Here's my card," the Skycap said.

"Nice card," I said. "How come it's in Japanese?"

"If you can't lick 'em," he said, "join 'em!"

The Japanese gentlemen was back again, bowing.

"Where's my sister-in-law?" I said.

"We can't get her out of the ladies' room—she's afraid of *you*."

"Ridiculous!" I said.

"That's what the ladies' room attendant told her, but she won't come out from under the sink."

"There's nothing to be afraid of—this is *America!*" I said, realizing instantly that this was the funniest line I had ever spoken.

The Japanese gentleman bowed again. I bowed again, and he left. The black Skycap passed, pushing a load of crushed "uncrushable" luggage; he stopped and bowed, murmuring a stage-whispered "We have nothing to fear but fear itself."

Then as in a burst of smoke, so it seemed, the Japanese gentleman reappeared, dragging a terrified tiny tub of a

Japanese girl. My sister-in-law—come all the way from Japan.

"Hello, Mitsue," I said, and I never should have bowed because when I straightened up, she had disappeared. And she wasn't in the ladies' room. A moment later there came a loud shriek from the men's room, and five terrified homosexuals, who had been caucusing there, fled wild-eyed toward the safety of a kindly narco cop, who had been loitering near the Customs Office in hopes of picking up a brassiere full of hashish from Hong Kong.

"I'll go get her," I told the no-longer-bowing Japanese gentleman.

I spotted my shy sister-in-law immediately. She was crouching inside a floor-length urinal, trying to look white and ceramic, hoping she wouldn't be noticed by the itinerant pissiers.

"Mitsue," I said, "this is America. There's nothing to be afraid of—"

"America," she said, looking around inside the urinal, "Lincoln Center?"

"Look," I said, "if you wanna see Reiko and the rest of America, you've got to come with me."

As soon as I said "Reiko" Mitsue's moon face took on a look of tentative trust. "Reiko?" she repeated.

"Yes," I said, "that's your sister. I'll take you to her."

Mitsue left the safety of the enveloping urinal and touched it gently, in a parting gesture. "Good-bye, Lincoln Center," she said. At that moment the receptacle flushed automatically. Mitsue reached out her hand again. "Don't cry," she said.

Reiko's sister, Mitsue, who had volunteered to help Reiko with the baby Timothy, Bobby, me, and the cooking and the housework, tried to fake it, but Reiko's sister, Mitsue, didn't know a goddamn thing about babies, Bobby, me, cooking, or housework. She could nimble-finger up a dandy kimono, an art she had studied in Japan, but after Reiko, Bobby, Timothy, and I had all the dandy kimonos we would ever need in this life and part of the next, there was a decided lull in her creative activity, or any activity. This little fat Japanese "mother's helper" became a vegetable. A very contented vegetable. She was up at dawn to decide what she wouldn't do that day, and at 8 P.M. she would try to move past me without being seen and vanish into her bedroom. Another satisfactory day well done.

Eating was one of the accomplishments she hadn't mentioned in her application for round-trip plane fare from Tokyo. Why round-trip, I couldn't fathom. She apparently had no intention of using the other half of her ticket. Not for air travel anyway.

Mitsue's appetite could be compared to someone in the Donner party on about the twenty-third day of being trapped by that Sierra blizzard. And I'm sure if breakfast, dinner, or lunch were a little late, she would have no compunction about a dash of cannibalism. She seemed devoted to Timothy, who was fat and juicy at that age, and every night before we nailed him in his little crib we counted his chubby little fingers and toes. We were always astounded when he seemed to have the correct number.

This was the extent of Mitsue's helping out. She carried Timothy around all day and part of the night. Of course, Timothy loved this, and just like Dr. Spock had written, in one of his lucid moments, this was a good way to spoil a baby. And that's what happened in no time. After a while, when Mitsue or Reiko, when it was her turn at bat, attempted to put Timothy down in order to go to the bathroom or some other unnecessary (Timothy reasoned) function, he screamed like a dying pig. Consequently, in the interests of peace and quiet and order, which I insist on at all times, Timothy became part of Mitsue's left hip. Maybe this is why she went to bed so early. To give her hip a chance to dry out.

Pussycat, our female cougar, came in heat along about the third or fourth month that Mitsue had been staying with us. For those of you who have never been around a female cougar in heat, as Jolson used to say, "You ain't heard nothin' till you hear a female cougar in heat!" Take all the Tarzan yells that were ever yelled and put them on the same sound track and turn the volume up to "Impossible," and that will give you some idea of the sounds she makes. This is the ultimate in female frustration (I'm speaking, of course, of the unavailability of a male cougar) or, to listen to poor Pussycat in her agony, a male "anything." She literally climbed the wall, or, more accurately, she ran around the walls of her cage like they were horizontal.

I don't know whether Pussycat's anguished desolation triggered Mitsue's undeveloped or incipient psyche, but she asked Reiko to get her a date.

Immediately we both tried to figure out what kind of a male cougar Mitsue would like. We decided on Ferd, the butcher's son. He was a certified public accountant. He wasn't too bad looking (I had heard), and he seemed to be a gentleman, and he went along with the idea. And he had a pickup truck which would come in handy, I ungallantly reminded Reiko, if Mitsue ran amuck at some McDonald's hamburger stand.

The big evening was a Saturday. When else in this well-ordered world? And from the moment Mitsue knew she had a locked-in date, she became dissatisfied with her entire wardrobe. The way she talked, as interpreted by Reiko, because Mitsue apparently had no intention of ever speaking English—not to me, anyway—I thought she was going to take the next plane out to Paris, spend a few days with Courreges or Givenchy. But it didn't happen this way. She settled for the local Shmatte Shoppe, which wasn't too far behind an Army and Navy Store when it came to the latest thing. That evening, after a day of frenzied indecision, Mitsue modeled her new clothes for me, Bobby, and Timothy.

The first thing she broke out was the coat she had bought because the weather had turned nippy. I couldn't believe it. I had never seen an evening mackinaw. I asked Reiko what it was, and Reiko, truthful as always, gave me a straight answer. She said it was a coat. From where I sat, it looked like a plaid shower curtain with a mouse fur collar glued to it. I told Reiko to tell Mitsue I was crazy about it. When Mitsue heard the news, she giggled happily. This, I must admit, told me nothing because no matter what happened, she always giggled happily. In my mind's eye I can see her in front of Pancho Villa's firing squad, just after she has been raped and ravished by Pancho's entire army, giggling happily.

"What is she gonna wear under the coat?" I wanted to know.

"Clothes," Reiko said, truthful as ever.

"Any particular kind of clothes?" I said.

"You'll see," Reiko said. And in a few moments Mitsue slinked—or is it slank?—out of the bedroom in another creation which was beyond belief. They were, apparently, fringe, with attached pajamas. The fringe was gold and the pajamas were red. She looked like something they gave to a volunteer fire department for winning the hosing contest at Nutmeg, Connecticut.

"Where's this kid Ferd taking her?" I said. "To a Druid meeting?"

"What's that?" Reiko said.

"Well," I started to explain, "it's a sort of an organization that used to pile big rocks on top of each other and they worshiped trees, and when all is said and done, there's really only one—Margie, Margic, it's you."

Reiko looked at me for a long time after this, and then sighing a deep Far Eastern sigh, she resigned herself and didn't continue this hopeless conversation. Mitsue said something in Japanese to Reiko and Reiko said something to Mitsue—in Japanese. I said something in Druid to Bobby and he said, "A big kid hit me on the school bus today."

"Don't take the school bus anymore," I said. "You're liable to get yourself killed."

"Can't I hit him back?" Bobby said.

"Sure," I said, "why not?"

"Because I'm liable to get myself killed," he said.

"I wouldn't want that to happen," I said. "Without you, who could I be a pal to?"

"This kid is eight feet tall," Bobby said. "His name is Pilsudski—he's in the fourth grade, he's Polish."

"How could he be eight feet tall in the fourth grade?" I said.

"Easy," Bobby said. "They've got very high ceilings."

Strange with children. Either they're innocently funny, or
they start putting you on at a very early age.

During this heartwarming exchange between a loving
father and son, Mitsue stood as if in a painful manikin
pose. Her pudenda shoved forward and her tiny bosoms
backed off, with her right toe pointed south-southwest and
her left toe indicating the direction of the magnetic pole.
In that red and gold outfit, she looked like she was model-
ing a deformed apple.

"How do you think she looks?" Reiko asked. "Do you
think Ferd will like her?"

"If he doesn't," I said, "we'll castrate him just to teach
him a lesson."

"What does that mean?" Reiko said, not really waiting
for an answer.

"Why is Pilsudski Polish, Poppa?" Bobby said.

"That's just a Polish name," I said. "That means his
parents, or his grandparents or maybe even his great-
grandparents came from Poland which is a country in
Europe where Polish people come from. But he's an American."

"I'm American," Bobby said, not without some pride, or
maybe I should say with a great deal of pride. He was so
happy about being an American, I felt sorry that we
weren't living back in the eighteenth century and the
Revolutionary War days. I'm sure Bobby would have been
a Green Mountain Boy, or a Nathan Hale, or a Pilsudski.

"Maybe she and Ferd will get married," Reiko said.

"Jesus Christ," I said. "They haven't even had their first
date and now you have them getting married. Why?"

"Because Mitsue wants to get married. That's what she
came to America for."

So now it was out. She didn't come to help out with
Timothy and our group. She came here to start her *own*
group.

"Don't you think she ought to look around a little?" I
said. "There must be other fish in the sea besides this
Ferd. He's not the only pebble on the beach."

"Mitsue doesn't want to marry a fishman," Reiko said.
"She could have married a fishman in Japan. They've got

plenty fishman in Japan, but Mitsue wants somebody who smells different."

"This Ferd is not a fishman," I said. "He's a certified public accountant."

"How do they smell?" Reiko said.

"Depends on how late they work at the office," I said, not quite knowing what this meant, but as always during our scrambled conversations, it didn't really matter. What mattered at the moment was Mitsue's new model wardrobe, which was to be road tested come Saturday night. And a new wardrobe, no matter if created by the elves in the Black Forest, could do little to improve Mitsue's figure, which came under the prolate spheroid classification. There was nothing that could be done. A Playtex 18-hour girdle would have quit in 15 minutes. And instead of a Maidenform bra, she could have used a cowboy belt. This didn't rule her out entirely in the nubility field, but on a clear day you could see the odds forever. Strange, how two sisters could be so different. Reiko has the most perfect of bodies and a lovely face, while Mitsue couldn't have won a beauty contest at an ostrich farm.

"Look," I said, "I think she looks lovely, and I'm sure this Ferd will be just crazy about her and her fringe." This seemed to satisfy Reiko and she told Mitsue the fashion show was over and Mitsue disappeared once more into her bedroom. I prayed that Ferd was just a little stupid and with as much vision as a mole.

"What does this Ferd look like?" I asked Reiko.

"I don't know," she said. "I never saw him. George, the butcher, just happened to mention that he had a son, who just got back from college, or somewhere, and he was just sort of hanging around."

"Why doesn't he help his father in the butcher shop?" I said.

"His father won't let him," Reiko said. "His father wants him to have all the things he never had."

"Like what?" I said.

"Like fingers," Reiko said. "George, the butcher's, only got two left on one hand and only three left on the other."

"Those meat-slicing machines," I said. "They're dangerous."

"That isn't how it happened," Reiko said. "Joan Simpson told me George, the butcher, was in Las Vegas, and that's how it happened. He was feeling up a slot machine for the fifty-dollar jackpot when all of a sudden it paid off. I don't understand."

I didn't understand either, but I'd think twice about feeling around with *any* of the equipment in Las Vegas. I mean, I still don't think, no matter what they say, that Bugsy Siegel died from natural causes.

After waiting for almost three whole days, Saturday finally came and with it, a little later, of course, came Saturday night, and Mitsue was ready. She had been ready at twelve noon and Ferd wasn't due until seven.

She went to the bathroom forty-seven times between noon and seven. I couldn't help counting because I thought we might have a new world's record right here in River City.

Ferd rolled to our door in his pickup truck at 7:15— giving Mitsue the longest fifteen minutes in her entire life. For her, it was like being left at the altar with unborn triplets. She thought Ferd wasn't going to show. After I saw him, I was afraid because he had. Professor Leakey has been looking in the wrong place.

Ferd had very little forehead. And his arms almost trailed the ground. I tried to see if his knuckles were nicked from our stone walk, but I wasn't successful, mainly because he kept his hands in his pockets, which were cut in the sides of his knees.

"Hello," I said, in my most charming welcome-to-the-family manner. "I'm Jack Douglas and this is Reiko and this is Bobby and this is Timothy and this is Mitsue." At that moment our young wolf squatted and released a lake all over the hall carpet.

"That dog there," Ferd said, "needs to be housebroke. Needs it real bad."

"That's a wolf," Bobby said.

"That wolf there," Ferd said, without breaking rhythm, "needs to be housebroke. Needs it real bad."

"His name is Tyrannosaurus Rex," Bobby, the Jolly Liar, said.

"That Tyrannosaurus Rex, there," Ferd said, with the same beat, "needs to be house—"

"I've been working on it," I said, knowing full well that if I worked on it from now until the next Ice Age, that wolf or any other would never be housebroken, anymore than you can sandbox train a Siberian tiger. You can get 'em to the box, but you can't make 'em—.

"This is Mitsue," Reiko said before the conversation got too animalistic.

"Pleased to meet you," Ferd said, with almost a curtsy. Where the hell did he pick that up? I thought. Mitsue just giggled, holding her hand over her mouth in the time-honored custom of all Oriental girls. Except Reiko. She never did that. I wonder why. Maybe she lied to me—maybe she's Swedish.

"I got the truck right outside," Ferd said. "Had it washed."

"It's pretty," I said, looking out the window. "It's a nice brown truck."

"That's beige," Ferd corrected me.

"That's a nice beige truck," I said, not wishing to foment any generation gap.

"Actually it's bamboo beige—that's what the feller at the used car lot called it," Ferd said.

"That's a nice bamboo-beige truck," I said, wishing to Christ we were still at Lost Lake and the only conversation I had to make was with my own little family, my animals, and the great spirit Manitou who watched over all of us forest dwellers.

"It's got four-wheel drive," Ferd said. "Gotta have four-wheel drive around these parts—goddamn city folks won't let us pave the roads."

"Well, now," I said, finding myself slightly nettled. "I'm not too much in favor of paving the roads either, and I'm not city folks. I'm strictly backcountry folks, and I think if you pave all the roads, you're gonna have a lot more traffic and motorcycle nuts and trucks and maybe even hitchhikers, and I think there's enough six-packs lining the sides of the roads now. Just think what it would be like if the roads were paved?"

"Maybe you're right," Ferd admitted, with some truculence, "but come winter—we get snow up here in the mountains—you'll see how tough it is to drive with three foot of snow on the ground on an unpaved road."

"We have ten feet of snow on the ground in Canada," Bobby said, "and we didn't have no trouble. No trouble at all."

"Did you have four-wheel drive?" Ferd wanted to know.

"We had a snowmobile," Bobby said. "It went like a bat outa hell!"

"Bobby!" Reiko said. "No say 'hell' in front of people—only in the family."

"Yeah," I said, "we like to keep hell in the family—gives us a nice feeling of togetherness."

By this time Ferd had lost interest in this maze of trivia and tales of the deep-snow country and had taken refuge in rolling a cigarette—something I hadn't seen anyone do since William S. Hart in *West of the Rio Grande and South of the Border and North of Bakersfield,* one of the first silents. Ferd had none of William S. Hart's expertise and managed to spill half a sack of Bull Durham onto our new carpet—just at the point the wolf had peed. This combination did something to the wolf, and he proceeded to rub his neck in it in the manner of all wolves when they sniff something particularly savory—not to us, but to a wolf. The wolf rubbed and rolled and groaned in ecstasy at this new blend he had discovered. Reiko, who frowned on anybody's urine or tobacco on our new carpet, suggested I take my goddamn wolf and escort him to the confines of his quarters. In order to avoid any unpleasantness in front of Ferd, I complied. I would have complied if Ferd hadn't been there, too, because with Reiko, the world is composed of strange odors—none of which she was aware of until she married me. Little did she know that she was getting a zoophilic husband as well as an ex-chorus boy.

Ferd finally gave up on trying to create a cigarette and

gave Bobby his nearly empty sack of Bull Durham and his box of cigarette papers. Bobby rolled one, right off. When I questioned him about this he said the devil made him do it. A likely story, but one I had to accept in front of Mitsue's future husband.

"Well," Ferd said, "I promised my ma I wouldn't smoke till I was forty-one, so it looks like I'm gonna keep my promise. We better get started."

"Have fun at the dance," I said.

"Oh, we will," Ferd said. "I can't dance."

On this ominous note, Ferd and Mitsue collided in the front doorway as Mitsue, Japanese-style, tried to let him go out first, and after the third try they got through the door and out to the bamboo-beige truck. After Mitsue held the door for Ferd, he got in and started the engine, gave an ear-shattering two toots on an air horn he must have stolen from a rude truck driver, and pulled out of our driveway.

"Gee," Reiko said, "I hope he doesn't get fresh with her."

"I thought that was the idea," I said.

"But Mitsue doesn't know about men," Reiko said.

"What is there to know?" I said. "Besides, that Ferd doesn't know too much about women, so they can start out together—even."

"Do you think he'd make a good husband for Mitsue?" Reiko said, leaving me with no hopeful answer. If I said what I thought, which was Ferd would make a great husband for someone who liked living in a tree, but I knew I couldn't say this to Reiko. She was genuinely concerned getting Mitsue married off, and so was I because I knew this would be the only reason she'd have for leaving our house (and going to live in a tree). But I didn't say what I thought. I said, "I think Ferd would make a fine husband for Mitsue, and if things don't work out, she can always sell him to the San Diego Zoo."

"What's that mean?"

"I mean it's better than getting shot out of a tree during the hunting season," I said, not meaning to. "At least at the zoo he'll be safe, and maybe he'll have his own rubber tire—to swing on."

Reiko turned to Bobby. "Your papa is a mean man," she said.

"I know," Bobby said. "He likes animals better than he does us." Then looking at me, on guard, he said, "That's what Mama said."

"I know," I said. "That's why I married Mama because I like animals better. Jesus Christ!"

"Are you gonna fight with Mama?" Bobby said.

"Why?"

"Because *Lost in Space* is on television and I wanna watch it!"

"We'll fight softly," I said.

At 2:00 A.M. we were jolted out of bed by the roar of Ferd's bamboo-beige pickup truck and by the avalanche of garbage cans sent roaring down the hill by the brush of the bamboo-beige snowplow attached to the front end of Ferd's bamboo-beige truck.

"Jack-san," Reiko said, nudging me into full consciousness, "I think the raccoons are after the garbage!"

"Sounds more like elephants," I said.

"Elephants?" she said. "I didn't know they had elephants in California."

"Well," I said, "they're on the endangered-species list, but—" It was then we heard the wild giggling of Mitsue, followed by a loud thump on the front door and apelike gurgling laugh.

"Missed ya," Ferd said. "Come on, give us a little kiss!" This followed by another jolting body blow against our front door.

"Missed again," I said. By this time Reiko and I were on the other side of the door, zeroing in with our radar.

"I hope she likes him," Reiko said. "And I hope he likes her."

"Come on!" Ferd mumbled.

"He likes *her*," I said.

"I'm from Japan," Mitsue said, defending her honor with a brave non sequitur.

"Mitsue doesn't know about men," Reiko said. "We better open the door and let her in."

"Why don't we just lock her out there and let her pick up a few pointers," I said.

"What does that mean?"

"It means that sooner or later Mitsue is going to have to get an education. Didn't your mother and father ever tell her anything?"

"They wanted her to marry Buddhist priest," Reiko said.

"I doubt very much if a Buddhist priest would have a bamboo-beige pickup truck," I said. "And that's very important."

"Come on, baby, give old Ferd a little smooch," from the other side of the door.

"I'm gonna let her in," Reiko said, trying to unbolt the front door and breaking one of her superlong fingernails.

"Wait a minute," I said. " 'Smooch' isn't what you think it is!"

"It's bad enough," Reiko said. "Mitsue doesn't know about men."

"She's twenty-four years old," I said. "Where has she been all her life?" Suddenly there was a loud scuffling sound accompanied by many thumps and scrapings, muffled voices, then all was quiet. Five seconds went by. Ten seconds. Fifteen seconds. After a half minute, Reiko couldn't stand it any longer and I was a bit curious too, so she unbolted the front door and flung it open, and there they were. Mitsue was flattened against a porch post, her arms in back of her, entwined around it. She looked like a vertical figurehead, carved on the bow of an old Japanese sailing ship, who was afraid of the water. Ferd was sitting on the porch steps optimistically starting to roll another cigarette. He held the cigarette paper in his left hand and a king-size sack of Bull Durham in his right. He poured the loose tobacco onto the paper like he was seasoning a pizza.

"Howdy, folks," Ferd said when we burst upon them—expecting to find an orgy and discovering we had unearthed a prayer meeting. "Been up trying to housebreak that there dog?"

"It's not a dog," Reiko said, her honesty bursting forth like measle spots. "It's a wolf."

"Tell ya what you do," Ferd said. "You get yourself a rolled-up newspaper, and every time you see that animal start to squat, you give him a good whack with that there rolled-up newspaper. That'll soon learn him."

"A friend of mine tried that with a wolf," I said, "and now they call my friend Lefty."

"I think I'm gonna be sick," Ferd said. "Goodnight, folks." With this he gave up on his Bull Durham project and lurched over to his bamboo-beige pickup truck, climbed into it, and slammed out of our driveway, taking a couple of newly planted rose trees with him.

"I hope he makes it home," Reiko said.

"I hope he doesn't," I said, my usual goodwill toward man surfacing.

Mitsue had quite a tale to tell, I learned through various and intermittent translation by Reiko. Ferd had taken her to dinner at a McDonald's hamburger stand and had gone all the way by ordering her a triple burger, with two orders of french fries and ketchup. Mitsue was very disappointed because McDonald's didn't serve soy sauce, or as the Japanese called it, shoyu sauce, which they put on everything, including Jell-o. I've tasted it on Jell-o because I didn't want the other kids to think I was chicken, and all I can say—it gave me a bad trip.

After McDonald's, Mitsue had to go to the bathroom but was too shy to excuse herself, so she suffered in silence at the Firemen's Ball, which was the next stop. The Firemen's Ball, a project of the Volunteer Fire Department of Hackettsville, was supposed to raise money for a new pumper, a project which had been in operation for many years, but no one had ever seen the new pumper. The old pumper was good enough was the opinion of many, and although the old pumper was more decorative than practical, it *did* look very professional standing close by a house which was rapidly burning to the ground.

The Hackettsville Firemen's Ball, plus the commendable

attempt at raising money, also turned out every year, apparently, as a very good place to get drunk charitably. The booze money was going for a good cause, everybody said, and the crap tables didn't do badly either, in spite of the local Mafia, which consisted of one Godfather (Irving Puzo) and two senile hoods who could no longer make it in the Brownsville section of Brooklyn and had been retired to Hackettsville, where they kept their hand in as best as they could. They sold protection to woodchucks. That really didn't amount to much, but running the crap tables annually at the Firemen's Ball enabled them to make a stake for the whole year. It was a 50-50 deal. The Hackettsville Fire Department got 50 percent of the 10 percent which Irving Puzo confidentially informed them was the 100 percent the crap tables brought in. This is why the Hackettsville Volunteer Fire Department was several million light-years away from its impossible dream of a new pumper.

There was a time when Irving Puzo tried to expand by adding craps to the Friday night bingo games in the church basement. But Father Luciano, whose family had originally come from Sicily, said that a few good Friday nights for Puzo and they might have to hock the Virgin Mary to pay off. Father Luciano was almost as wise as Barry Fitzgerald.

Mitsue, who still hadn't gone to the bathroom, had had to dance every dance with Ferd. She told Reiko it was agony. Not only did she have to pee, but Ferd only knew one step, which included a low dip, and this dangerously tilted her kidneys. Also, she said, no matter what tune the three-piece band would play, Ferd would always sing. "Shine On, Harvest Moon." Which made, apparently, for the ultra in agonized counterpoint—even to Japanese ears accustomed to years of quarter-tone dissonance.

"Why doesn't Mitsue go to the bathroom now?" I said. Reiko quickly jabbered something in Japanese to Mitsue, and Mitsue jumped up and ran.

"Looks like it's not gonna work," I said.

"What do you mean?" Reiko said.

"Mitsue and Ferd," I said. "She doesn't like him."

"Oh no?" Reiko said. "She's *crazy* about him—she says he smells just like the teahouse of the August moon."

"What the hell does that mean?" I said.

"I don't know how to say it in English," Reiko said. "You better go downhill and pick up garbage cans."

On my way down the hill, I thought about it—might be nice to have a brother-in-law who smelled like the teahouse of the August moon. Maybe no one would notice he looked like Snowflake, the albino gorilla.

I wish I could say that Mitsue gradually changed into the Admirable Crichton and became a treasured member of our little antisocial group, but it didn't happen that way. Outside of toting Timothy around night and day, she accomplished nothing in any other direction. She didn't learn how to cook rice, or feed Timothy, or shoe a horse (which wasn't one of our requirements, but it would have exposed a glimmer of responsibility and initiative and originality). We had to face it—Mitsue was a vegetable, whose only apparent destiny was to be a small gumbo in the mulligan stew of life. She couldn't, or didn't care to, participate in anything resembling toil. We suggested she get herself a job because she wanted to stay in America. She was all for this until we arranged a few interviews with some unwary employers, then she would plead a sick headache, or she was going back to the old country and marry a Buddhist priest. As soon as the dark shadow of honest employment had dissipated her headache disappeared, and the bachelor Buddhist priest in Japan was left with his empty beads and his lonely tom-toms.

Ferd had never come back, and no one in Hackettsville has seen him since the night of the Firemen's Ball. We don't know if he accidentally ran his bamboo-beige pickup truck over a cliff somewhere, or he kept right on driving like a loner lemming until he reached the sea. Mitsue never mentioned him, but Reiko said it was the Poor Butterfly bit all over again.

As the weeks became months and the months became years and the years became epochs, Mitsue stayed on with us. Eating. She ate herself into a globe. She looked like a weather balloon. If only she were, we could have waited for a good windy day and sent her aloft. That way she might have met some nice boy in Greenland. But the wind never got strong enough for this wishful project.

Reiko got her dates, but things never worked out. They were either too tall or too short or too quiet or too noisy or too everything. Finally they were too few. Then there were none. It was sad. Mitsue had never forgotten Ferd. Then one day God, in His mercy, sent Mitsue another bamboo-beige pickup truck driven by a short, miserable-looking man, who happened to be looking for a Christmas tree (the people who had formerly owned our property grew and sold them). I could never sell any of our Christmas trees because they looked so beautiful in the snow, but after this little man saw Mitsue, he didn't care. He'd changed his mind about what he wanted for Christmas. And Mitsue seemed similarly struck—to her, this ugly little bastard was Gregory Peck, Charlton Heston and Mick Jagger all rolled into one. And that's the way he looked—as if they had taken those three and put them into a used car crusher and this was the result.

We didn't see Mitsue much after that fruitful day. She was always somewhere with Milt. Milt Bellringer. That was his name and he had a dairy farm in Hackettsville. And maybe the only solvent dairy farm left in California. Most of the others have sold their cows to the highest dog-food bidder and gone into the real estate business.

Mitsue seemed to spend most of her time with Milt at his dairy farm. One slight accidental incident had almost wrecked an otherwise perfect potential union. Milt had shown Mitsue how to milk the cows by machine, of course, and apparently she understood the mechanics, if that is the right word, of thoroughly washing the cow's udder and attaching the nozzles of the milking machine to the cow's teats, and just how long to let the machine run. With Mitsue to help him, Milt could get the rest of his chores done much faster and have more time for her. This was the theory, and everything seemed to go as planned until one evening Mitsue became absorbed in the Japanese *Reader's Digest*—with a condensed version of *The Pil-*

grim's Progress (which took *some* condensing)—and left the milking machine attached to the cows a little too long. When Milt came back into the barn, the cows had long since run out of liquid, and they just stood there, helplessly, their cheeks gradually being drawn inward as the machine sucked on, without mercy. The cows looked like they were lined up waiting to be kissed by Paul Newman. Milt let out a scream when he saw his precious Holsteins on the verge of being bagged by their own udders, and shut off the power. The cows, all fifty of them, sighed in unison, causing a down draft which flipped a Piper Cub which was cruising at an illegal altitude.

Mitsue's romance survived because the herd did, but it was the acid test of any dairy-type romance. The cows came first, which upon contemplation is the way it should be. Without milk there would be no civilization, so it isn't Russia we have to worry about—it's Borden's.

Some months after Milt had been squiring Mitsue around Hackettsville and the Bakersfield Fair and other fun spots of the Western world, at Reiko's insistence, abetted by my curiosity, I asked Milt about his future intentions.

"Well," he said, in his best yokel imitation, "I think I'll add a few Jerseys to the herd. They don't give as much milk but it's very rich. Very, very rich."

"What about Mitsue?" I said.

"I dunno," Milt said, rekindling the rubber bands he was smoking in his all-weather meerschaum. "I sorta had my heart set on Jerseys."

I knew I was going to get an answer like this, so I don't know why I was irritated, but I felt, as Mitsue's patron saint, I had a right to know—and soon.

"I like your sense of humor, Milt," I said, "but if you don't do something about Mitsue, we're going to have to ship her back to Japan and a Buddhist priest who's got a hot kimono for her back there in Kyoto."

"You mean Charlie Matsuoka?" Milt said. "Mitsue told me about him. She said she don't wanna marry no Buddhist priest nohow."

"Well," I said, trying to maneuver downwind from

Milt's polluted pipe, "she's gotta marry somebody, and if you like cows better than her——"

"I didn't say that," Milt said quickly, inadvertently knocking a few fire arrows from his pipe into the left breast pocket of his windbreaker, which had not been flameproofed, and in a few moments Milt's left breast was smoldering. Milt, whose reactions were slightly slower than a retarded sloth, did nothing. "Your left breast is on fire," I said.

"I know," Milt said, "but I'm too shy to tell her."

"No, no," I said, "it's your *windbreaker*—your *pipe* set it on fire."

"Jesus Christ," Milt said, "talk about lousing up a mood. Goddamn pipe sets everything afire!" He immediately shook up a bottle of Coke and neatly extinguished his left breast. Then he knocked his pipe against the wall of the barn into some loose hay and in no time at all the barn had burned to the ground.

"Good day for a fire" was Milt's only comment to the reporter from the Hackettsville *Times*, "no wind."

"How'd the fire start, Mr. Bellringer?" persisted the reporter, who was new at it.

"Vandals," Milt said.

I felt that during a barn burning down wasn't quite the right moment for delicate romantic questions about my little sister-in-law's future, so I waited until Milt came over one Saturday night. I got him alone, gave him a triple bourbon and Coke, and backed him into a corner.

"Are you going to marry Mitsue?" I asked bluntly.

"Yeah," Milt said. "Just as soon as my mother dies."

"What does that mean?"

"Well, I promised my mother that I wouldn't get married until she died," Milt said, offering his glass for another six fingers of bourbon.

"How old is your mother?" I said.

"Seventy-eight," Milt said.

"Oh," I said. "Then it looks like the wedding might be soon." I felt that this was a rather rude observation, but at seventy-eight, I knew she couldn't be out playing polo. "Where's your mother now?" I said.

"I dunno," Milt answered. "She left the house this morning before I did. Took her pony and her mallet." All my life I've been wrong.

"That sounds like a joke," I said.

"Mr. Douglas," Milt said, again indicating he'd like his bourbon replenished, and promptly, "to you, *everything* sounds like a joke. That's your racket. Making jokes about any- and everything. Right?"

"In a way," I said. "But, this Mitsue business is very serious and I'm sure she doesn't want to wait until your mother dies to get married. Besides, the whole thing makes it seem like Mitsue's wanting to get married is sort of pressurizing your mother a little bit."

"Don't you worry about Old Mumsie," Milt said, mellowing now considerably after his third triple bourbon. "Old Mumsie isn't going to be pushed into doing anything she doesn't want to do."

"Does she drive a car?" I said, grasping at straws.

"Yeah."

"On the Ridge Route?"

"Yeah."

"When it's raining?"

"Yeah." This was some comfort. The law of averages would certainly take care of Old Mumsie, I was sure. Some dark wet night, Old Mumsie would be barreling up from the city on the Ridge Route, and the fiftieth driver would be doing the same thing in the opposite direction— in the same lane as Old Mumsie (according to the Allstate Insurance Company ads, one driver in fifty is drunk)— and this slight coincidence would take care of Old Mumsie and pave the way for an immediate East-West nuptial happening. And this would be none too soon because I thought that Mitsue was more than a little pregnant although she was so round it was hard to tell, except that she looked a little rounder than usual in one area. She looked like a weather balloon that had swallowed a basketball.

I wish I could give this chapter on Reiko's little sister a happier ending but that would be dishonest. Mitsue did not marry Milt Bellringer. Milt Bellringer married his mother upon the advice of his psychiatrist, whose philosophy about problems was to give them another name. So Milt got rid of his Oedipus complex by making his mother his wife. She was still his mother, but instead of Old Mumsie, he now called her Baby. The whole thing sounded very unsavory to me, but they'll probably make a dandy movie out of it.

Mitsue, heartbroken, took off and went to live in Hawaii, where she immediately fell in love with a beach boy who owned a bamboo-beige surfboard.

18

WITH the exception of a few quick and painful trips to Hollywood and the office of Johnny Blackwell, which had become the Forest Lawn of Fun, for more of what were now known as *strategic* story conferences, to figure out what should be done with *The Devil and the Hot Virgin,* Reiko and I had settled down to living what is known as a normal life, in a normal American community.

Bobby was attending a regular school with regular children and rapidly losing his childish naïveté and wonderment of the world, which he had had plenty of back in the bush. Timothy spent most of the day trying to demolish all our pots and pans, plus falling downstairs a lot.

Reiko was prepared to live this way from now on, but I spent most of my spare time poring over some of the splendid color photographs I had taken of our now-lost Lost Lake dream home.

The pictures I took in the wintertime were the most intriguing and never failed to instill a great longing in my vitals. The main lodge with its shiny yellow peeled log walls, its heavy shake roof and the brilliant red-painted doors against a background of the whitest of snows and the bluest of skies always gave me a jolt of pure homesickness. I marveled that a place I had known for only such a comparatively short time could have, out of all the places I have lived in life, become a home. Just that. Home.

Our *new* house was finished, but it needed something—like furniture, carpeting and a smaller mortgage; so at the prodding insistence of Reiko, who never believed I did any work at all, ever, I took her suggestion that I look around for something to augment my apparently lifetime weekly stipend from the Johnny Blackwell project with an infinitesimal mini-measure of good grace. Actually, I did nothing in this direction but just waited for the telephone to ring—with a long-distance call from Opportunity. In a week or so, this is exactly what happened.

I was romping with the young wolf, whom I had named Tanuki II, and was trying to let him know that playtime was over, when Reiko called me into the house. Leaving half of my brand-new windbreaker with Tanuki II, who didn't accept the termination of playtime too readily, I trudged up the hill from the wolf pen to the house.

Opportunity was on the phone in the form of the personal manager of Miss Obnoxious. An alleged comedienne, Miss Obnoxious was a fat, short, unabashedly unattractive "broad" (a word I abhor, but the only one which fits this particular case). Miss Obnoxious, strange as it seemed to me, was headed for oblivion. I could see nothing in her personality or her delivery or her sense of what was funny. She did all the obvious jokes about her fat and unappetizing personality, but I felt that she didn't really believe that she was what she was. I think that she felt as if she were Helen of Troy making these things up to get a few laughs.

I was contacted by her manager, who felt he was her Svengali, and I've never yet met a manager who didn't feel this way about his client—and why they call them clients instead of patients I'll never know, but anyway— This manager, Harry Kalb by name, wanted me to drive up to a Lake Tahoe mountain resort where she was appearing one weekend, to see how she worked.

"Can't we avoid all that?" I said to Harry Kalb on the phone. "I've seen her on television—I know how she works."

"In a nightclub it's different," Harry said.

"How could it be different?" I said. "Is she suddenly gonna work like Mitzi Gaynor, or Joey Heatherton, or Clint Eastwood?"

"That's sarcasm," Harry said perceptively.

"No, it isn't, Harry. She can get dirty in a nightclub, but

her delivery isn't going to be any different, and she's still going to do fat jokes and ugly jokes and what's going to be different, and, besides, although I can see the mountains from here, Lake Tahoe must be a good five-hour drive—and on a *weekend!* Jesus!"

"You sound like you don't like Sallie," he said, half sad and half bristly.

"That's silly," I said. "How could anyone not like Sallie?" Thinking as I said it, how could anyone in the whole wide world have a spark of *anything* for this repellent heifer, including her mother?

"Then you'll come up to Tahoe and see her?" Harry asked. "She's gonna appear at Kerry's Kimeeko Lodge."

"I've never heard of it," I said.

"You'll love Kerry's Kimeeko Lodge," he said. "They got everything!"

"Like what?" I said, growing more and more disenchanted with the prospect of writing anything for somebody I didn't give a damn about—although I had done it before.

"Do you play golf?" Harry said.

"No."

"Tennis?"

"No."

"Horseback riding?"

"No."

"How about archery, trap shooting, dancing, dining, drinking, ice skating, motorboating, losing weight, or bingo?"

"Yes," I said.

"Yes—to what?" Harry said.

"Yes, I'll come up to Kerry's Kimeeko Lodge," I said. "You make it sound so Christ-awful I wanna see it."

Reiko, after I begged her on bended knee and promised her more spices for her spice cabinet, agreed to feed the dogs, puma, and wolf, which left me free to drive to the once lovely Lake Tahoe.

Kerry's Kimeeko Lodge, rising out of the pine-cloaked slopes of northern California like an expensive Brasilia, is

both astounding and unbelievable in its turned-on chrome
and glass modernity. If this is a lodge, then the Taj Mahal
is a guesthouse. I was glad I came. And the reception I received from the lodge people was for the return of the
Messiah, but it was all for me. Kerry's Kimeeko Lodge
was a Jewish resort, and the warmth of a Jewish welcome
can never be surpassed or doubted. Here are a people who
are not afraid of showing their affections—probably the
only people, with the exception, maybe, of the Italians
who are capable of letting themselves go without a re-
straint. I knew I was among friends with the exception of
one; Harry Kalb, as Queen Victoria a few years back, was
not amused.

"Come on," Harry Kalb said, "I gotcha a room."

"A room?" I said. "You mean—*one* room?"

"Yeah," Harry said with some uncertainty. "One room."

"How can I entertain in one lousy room?" I said.
"Harry, dear boy, I must have a suite—or one of those
adorable cottages I saw on the way in."

"Jesus Christ," Harry said, "do you know how much a
suite—or a cottage—costs in the joint?"

"What does it matter," I said, "so long as it's adorable
and I'm happy, so I can think of what to do about Sallie
Landeau." (I knew what to do about her, but why
shouldn't I get a good night's rest? And who knows?
Maybe I *would* find someone to entertain—or vice versa.)

Harry was numbed by this request, but he walked back
to the desk and made arrangements for the Presidential
Suite, which was lovely and overlooked the Kimeeko
Lodge championship golf course and the Kimeeko Olym-
pic-size swimming pool and some very zoftic lovelies in
Band-Aid bikinis.

I didn't see the Queen of Comedy all day because she
was busy resting for her evening performance. Why she
should rest up for the night she was going to die I didn't
know. I just hoped I wouldn't be asked to eat anything at
the Kimeeko Rajah's Palace Nightclub before the show
because I wasn't too sure I could keep it down while
watching the Ton of Fun entertain the multitude with her
funny patter and off-key songs.

Harry Kalb must have been resting all day, too, because I didn't see him. I called the desk a few times and left messages like: "Mr. Kalb, please call Wasserman." Lew Wasserman, a lifelong friend of mine, I am proud to say (because I don't have many lifelong friends), was the head of Universal Studios in Hollywood. Then I put the number 213-452-6600 in the message, hoping that Harry Kalb would jump to conclusions and call this Hollywood number which was Wasserman's number all right, but it was *Doctor* Wasserman's number. This was a childish practical joke, but what the hell else was I going to do all that time in a $200-a-day suite at Kimeeko Lodge? Read the Gideon Talmud?

Showtime finally arrived and, until the "star" came on stage in the huge theater-restaurant of the Kimeeko Lodge, was very entertaining. They had a rock group, a juggler and an Arab tumbler, who really didn't click, and who had the good sense to keep tumbling after his act was over until he reached the safety of his Volkswagen and the open road.

At exactly ten o'clock came the announcement we all had been waiting for: "And now, ladies and gentlemen, the moment we all have been waiting for. Your favorite and mine, Miss Sallie Landeau!" The audience, apparently in a holiday mood and looking forward to the fun after the show, responded very well as Sallie clomped out to the microphone, diamonds or something shiny flashing like fire from every finger, and egret feathers in her hair.

She waited until the audience settled their drinking glasses; then she began with what she thought was an act. Her material was reminiscent of every female performer who had ever lived, from Sophie Tucker to Totie Fields, which she delivered in a south Bronx accent which made Buddy Hackett sound like Rex Harrison. Her songs were strangely enough on key—not always the key the orchestra was playing in, but close enough—and as a gesture to the younger generation, she threw in a rock number and did her version of today's "now" rock movements. They may have been plain and correct in her mind, but they didn't come out that way in the flesh. She looked like she was being manipulated by a spastic puppeteer. This number, which was her big finish, did very well. Everyone in the huge audience applauded vigorously because, I imagine, they had to do something to release the shock of seeing Sallie, the singing hassock, suddenly become Sallie, the dancing whale. The shock of the applause brought Sallie back for more encores than anyone except a mother would tolerate. She wore her audience so thin that after her last number she was the only one applauding.

After Sallie had retired to the wings, Harry Kalb beamed, "Isn't she exciting? Let's go back to the dressing room." This suggestion saved me from becoming an alcoholic starting at that moment. I don't ordinarily drink anything stronger than Jell-o which hasn't set, but in times of stress, like an evening with Sallie Landeau, I make an exception. If anyone had offered me a fix as we were leaving the table and heading backstage, I would have accepted it, although I don't ordinarily shoot anything stronger than Jell-o which hasn't set.

Sallie, in her dressing room, looked like an unattractive toad who had a tendency to sweat.

"You were sensational! Absolutely *sensational* tonight!" Harry Kalb said in a voice that seemed to be sliding up the scale. "Wasn't she sensational, Jack?"

"Yes," I heard myself saying, "sensational."

"Jack's the great comedy writer I was telling you about," Harry Kalb said, apparently feeling that he should explain about me before Sallie got the idea that I was the Avon lady, or maybe the Kimeeko Lodge termite inspector.

"He writes great jokes," Harry said.

"Really?" Sallie said, inspecting her meticulously manicured dirty fingernails. "Who'd you work for?"

"Well," I began, sensing the atmosphere of rejection, "there was Carmen Lombardo and Lawrence Welk, and I did a couple of routines for John Foster Dulles."

"He's just kidding," Harry Kalb nervously cut in.

"I don't do jokes," Sallie said, mopping her wet forehead with a handful of Kleenex.

"Nobody does," I said.

"And I don't do dirty material."

"What about that joke, I mean—what you said about the lesbian and the faggot on their wedding night?"

"Oh," Sallie said, "that. That's a slice of life. That could actually happen."

"Yeah," Harry Kalb said, "that's a truism."

"It's also dirty," I said, "and you need dirty material in a nightclub."

"I don't wanna be playin' nightclubs for my whole career," Sallie said. "I belong in the theater—or motion pictures—or maybe I could do a television series like *Julia*."

"Yeah," Harry said, "Sallie would be great in a series like *Julia*—she's got warmth. And she's exciting!"

A warm, exciting toad, I thought—maybe that's just what television needed.

"What kind of material would you like?" I said, trying to keep the farewell-forever tone out of my voice.

"I wanna kid about how sexy I am," Sallie said. "The women really go for that because then they know that I'm not a menace to their men. You can't be a menace and have the women like you."

"That's right," Harry brilliantly agreed.

Suddenly the whole thing was sad. Here was this monster of something almost female who wanted to make fun of herself as a sex symbol, but she didn't believe, deep in her heart, she was as much of a chimera as she unfortunately was. She could look into a mirror and see not a truck driver in drag but Raquel Welch. I knew then I couldn't write anything for her. And as much as we could have used a home improvement windfall of some sort, I couldn't take the money and give her the only kind of tired routine she could handle. No matter what, she would never improve, either in her delivery or her appearance. Sallie Landeau was doomed to play theater-restaurants in the mountains forever.

Two weeks after I decided all this, Sallie Landeau was signed by a network for a TV series similar to *Julia*.

Years ago I also turned down Lucille Ball and Desi Arnaz when they came up with the idea of *I Love Lucy*.

19

ALTHOUGH I made no deal with Harry Kalb and his horrendous client, my trip to Tahoe was well worthwhile because while enjoying the hospitality of Kerry's Kimeeko Lodge, I met a man worthwhile— Smiling Al of the CBDO & DF advertising agency. Smiling Al, a happily married man, had come up to Kerry's Kimeeko Lodge because he thought Kerry's Kimeeko Lodge was featuring a Singles Weekend that particular Friday, Saturday and Sunday, which wasn't true; but Smiling Al had decided, he informed me confidentially, to stay on and see what turned up. What turned up was me, which wasn't quite what he had in mind, but talking to me in the bar gave him a chance to case the room for something else.

After the second martini, we were lifelong friends. I'm usually a lifelong friend after the first martini, but in Smiling Al's case it took a little longer because he really wasn't smiling. He was showing his teeth, with a twinkle.

Smiling Al told me he was in charge of commercials at CBDO & DF and asked me if Reiko and I had ever done any. We haven't, so after the fourth martini, Smiling Al all but signed us up for one. I'm sure if he had had a contract in the inside pocket of his velvet hunting jacket (with the lace cuffs and the leopard-skin-reinforced elbows), he would have insisted on my signature. Nothing like this happened, and after the sixth martini (his), I felt that in the morning he would forget all of the night before and wonder where he had been and who he had been with, but this was not the case. Two weeks after I had met Smiling Al in the Oak Room of Kerry's Kimeeko Lodge, he called

me in Hackettsville and asked me if I would mind driving
to Hollywood the next day to meet the rest of his ad
agency and two Japanese gentlemen who were in the
United States to buy a little TV time to advertise their
food product: Mamma Mia's Sukiyaki. This was a pretty
weird-sounding brand name to my Western ears, but
somehow, after a once-upon-a-time trip to Rome, Mr.
Toki Yamoda and Mr. Yukio Kyushu had gotten their
Italian and English mixed with their mother tongue. It
sounded beautiful and very marketable, and maybe they
were right. That's why Reiko and I drove to Hollywood
because of a chance of doing a commercial, which is the
shortest cut to wealth, independence, and freedom from
want and insulting billets-doux from the Diner's Club,
whose bookkeeping system does not allow for *their* mistakes—only ours.

The conference with Mr. Yamoda and Mr. Kyushu, and
Charlie, Bill and Smiling Al of the CBDO & DF advertising agency proceeded about as smoothly as the peace talks
between Geronimo and the U.S. Cavalry. Smiling Al never
stopped smiling, but I knew that, inside, the lining of his
stomach was feeding on itself. With relish.

At this first meeting Mr. Yamoda spoke English of a
sort and acted as an interpreter for Mr. Kyushu. (At a
subsequent meeting it was the other way around. Apparently they had forgotten who was playing which part.)

It is difficult enough to explain to an American sponsor
just what you are going to do to sell his product, especially
if there is any humor or comedy connected with it; and
also it is difficult to explain to a sponsor *who* the actors
are who are going to sell his product. No matter if you
have been on television for thirty years for eight hours a
day, they won't know who you are. Apparently all a sponsor watches on television is his own commercials. Everything else, to him, is just the icing on the cake—or the
black border around a death announcement card.

Smiling Al, who seemed to be in charge (at ad agencies
even to come close to guessing who's in charge is a major
triumph) patiently explained to the two inscrutable
gentlemen from the land of the rising sun that Reiko and I

were going to do a 15-second, a 30-second and a 60-second hilariously funny skit extolling the virtues of Mamma Mia's Sukiyaki. These three hysterical bits which were to be written by me, the famous Jack Douglas, America's most beloved humorist and hilarious 15-, 30-, and 60-second skit writer. The skits would be performed by Reiko, America's most beloved singer , dancer, actress *and* mother, and me.

In the first place, only at this initial meeting did I get this kind of news. I didn't know that I had been chosen out of the thousands of America's most beloved humorists to be so honored, and, secondly, I didn't know whether I could be very goddamn humorous in 15 seconds. Of course, I gave no sign that this came as a total surprise. I just beamed enigmatically as Smiling Al's secretary sponged my white-on-white face with a cold damp cloth, while Smiling Al informed the potential sponsors that I had a hang-up. Whenever I thought of anything tremendously funny, I was so overwhelmed by the genius-like cleverness of it all that I slipped into a catatonic state. He also told them it was nothing to be alarmed about and all beloved American humorists were plagued by this same harmless condition, which was all part of being America's most beloved humorist. Smiling Al made the whole thing sound like a package deal. Catatonia and humor. Smiling Al might have been closer to the truth than he realized at that moment.

There's something about doing business with an Oriental which is quite frustrating to most Caucasians. The Oriental never commits himself, and so as our little meeting progressed and Smiling Al kept repeating his pitch to these two producers of Mamma Mia Sukiyaki, in so many different ways and with the most odd and picturesque phraseology, I began to have great respect for his ingenuity; as outlandish and weird as some of the twists he gave his pitch were, his capacity for invention seemed limitless. I couldn't help thinking, as people used to say about Willie Sutton: if only he had applied his great talent to legitimate purposes, who knows what heights he might have attained! He could have been another Billy Graham.

I was so admiring of Smiling Al's extemporaneous soliloquy I missed its impact on Mr. Yamoda and Mr. Kyushu. When I finally checked up on what effect Smiling Al was having on them, I couldn't believe it was the same two smiling, bowing gentlemen of a couple of hours ago. Now they weren't just inscrutable—they were cast in *bronze*.

"Al," I said, with as much empathy as I could muster up for this slicker, "maybe you'd better get Sessue Hayakawa and Anna May Wong—I don't think these guys are gonna buy us."

"On the contrary," Mr. Yamoda said, "you are already—as you put it—bought. What remains is Mamma Mia's Sukiyaki. How will we get the American people to buy this delic-ci-ous production—in quantity?"

Smiling Al, who had been ready to give up and fall on his own sword, jumped from his seat and almost screamed, "We could say, 'You don't have to be Japanese to enjoy Mamma Mia's Sukiyaki.' "

"Ah so," Mr. Yamoda said, "like 'You don't have to be Jewish to enjoy Levy's Rye Bread.' Same same—no?"

"Well," Smiling Al said, caught neatly in his own big fat trap, "yes, it is a little like the Levy's Rye Bread commercial, but with a twist."

"What twist?" Mr. Kyushu said, opening his mouth for the first time and in English, yet.

"Well," Smiling Al said, "for one thing we are not selling a Jewish product. To Jewish people. We are selling a Japanese product to all kinds of people—"

"What twist?" Mr. Kyushu said.

"How about Anna May Wong and Louie Prima?" I said.

"Please, Jack," Smiling Al said, baring his fangs like a strong timber wolf pursuing an enfeebled old moose, "I'm trying to show Mr. Kyushu and Mr. Yamoda that with this fabulous campaign I have planned, or, I should say, we here at the shop have planned, Mamma Mia's Sukiyaki will by this time next year be on every breakfast table in America!" Then Smiling Al turned and beamed his brightest on Mr. Kyushu and Mr. Yamoda.

Mr. Yamoda and Mr. Kyushu beamed back and both said, "What twist?"

I thought this would break Smiling Al, but it didn't, although he hesitated momentarily and lit a cigarette to give him pause, then he said, "I think what we need right now is a chart." Then he shouted like a deckhand on a Greek purse seiner, "Miss Marmelstein! Bring in the charts!"

Miss Marmelstein, who looked exactly like Elliott Gould, brought in an armful of rolled papers and dumped them, rather brusquely, I thought, on top of the untidy black mahogany conference table. Smiling Al shoveled back a small moraine of cigarette ash and spread one of the charts for all to see. Smiling Al's assistants, Charlie and Bill, were tremendously interested, but Mr. Kyushu and Mr. Yamoda didn't even glance up. Undismayed, Smiling Al launched into a lengthy explanation of what each chart meant, and what each chart meant was that Smiling Al would slash his wrists if he didn't get the Mamma Mia Sukiyaki account.

The second step in Smiling Al's all-out gut twister to secure the signatures of the masters of Mamma Mia Sukiyaki was a cocktail party. This, I presume, was designed to make Mr. Yamoda and Mr. Kyushu loosen up enough to sign *anything.*

The party was held in the dungeon room of a Beverly Boulevard Tower-of-London Tavern, which was a switch on the now-kicked idea of a real English pub in the heart of Los Angeles. The dungeon room was charmingly decorated by some gay decorator who went all out to make it a real dungeony dungeon. The walls were covered with chains and manacles and messages from former prisoners and, I suspect, from former customers who had been so rash as to eat the food. Water dripped from the ceiling as it does in all reputable dungeons, and mildew covered everything, including the waiters, who in the dim light of this fun room seemed to have Spanish moss instead of hair. The bald waiters had Spanish verdigris.

When Reiko and I arrived, we were greeted with much Smiling Al enthusiasm and were duly bussed and caressed

by the alcoholic trade wind of Smiling Al's breath. Smiling
Al seemed to be hitting the bottle hard of late. His frustration of not getting the Mamma Mia Sukiyaki account
signed and sealed was beginning to lead him down the
primrose path to the observation ward at the Cedars of
Lebanon Hospital. But Smiling Al was beyond caring. I
knew that if he didn't convince Mr. Yamoda and Mr.
Kyushu that Smiling Al's advertising campaign would
make Mamma Mia Sukiyaki a household word, he would
certainly create another incident to involve the United
States in another conflict with Japan. At times when he
was deepest in his cups and thinking lucidly, he would re-
veal his reprisal plan (if Yamoda and Kyushu didn't come
through): He would, he said, rent a Piper Cub at the
Honolulu airport, then he would fly over and drop a bag-
ful of cherry bombs on Don Ho. When I protested that
this not only might *not* create an incident, but might pro-
voke a vote of thanks, he was crushed and asked me if I
knew of an opium den in the neighborhood? Booze was no
longer enough.

The cocktail party had been under way for about two
and a half hours, and the guests of honor, Mr. Yamoda
and Mr. Kyushu, had not arrived. Reiko confided to us
that Japanese businessmen are never on time for anything—except their Christmas bonus.

This Operation Overwhelm party seemed to have about
reached its climax, and I felt sure that if the guests of
honor did not arrive soon, things would start going downhill, and what had been a congenial group of mutually interesting (to themselves) individuals might break up into
belligerent factions—the drunks versus the almost-drunks.
This had nothing to do with whether the honored guests
showed up or not. This was just the natural progression of
any cocktail party, no matter what the occasion. The best
defense against civil war at these affairs is the hors
d'oeuvres—but there have to be plenty and they have to
be filling, so there's not so much martini room in whatever part of our bodies takes care of food and booze.
Smiling Al's cocktail party had plenty of filling hor
d'oeuvres, but the people he had invited, plus their gate-

crashing friends, had no intention of eating. They had come to get pissed.

At 8:45, on the button, Mr. Yamoda and Mr. Kyushu showed up. Smiling and bowing and generally acting Japanese. They couldn't have been more honored. Even when some lovely young thing, with one breast bobbing out, did a mock bow upon meeting them and spilled a Bloody Mary all over Mr. Yamoda's white suit. He just smiled and bowed to the lovely young thing. Then he smiled and bowed to Smiling Al, who smiled and bowed back, knocking over a service table piled high with dirty glasses. Smiling Al turned and smiled and bowed to the service table at the same time his prominent rear unpremeditatedly nudged the lovely young thing's prominent rear, which caused her to lurch forward and spill a fresh Bloody Mary all over Mr. Kyushu's white suit. Mr. Kyushu smiled and bowed to the lovely young thing and then Mr. Kyushu and Mr. Yamoda smiled and bowed to each other and left the party.

For months Reiko and I took that long, boring drive down the Ridge Route to Hollywood to attend meetings and cocktail parties, theater parties, grand balls at the Ambassador and other festive functions in order to help Smiling Al sew up the Mamma Mia Sukiyaki account. Finally, I had to say to Smiling Al, whose hair was now snow white and patchy, "Al, I think we'll stay in Hackettsville for a while—we have a home there."

"But you *can't!*" Smiling Al said. "You and Reiko are going to do the commercials for Mamma Mia Sukiyaki! I *need* you! Mamma Mia *needs* you!"

"I know," I said, "but Mr. Yamoda and Mr. Kyushu don't need us—they can get Roy Rogers and Dale Evans and Anna May Wong."

"Wait a minute," Smiling Al said, his eyes bright with the star shell of a new thought. "Maybe you've got something there. Roy and Dale and Anna May Wong—East meets West at home on the range—"

"Anna May Wong died in 1961," Reiko said, astounding me with a correct fact.

"It might work," Smiling Al said. "It just might work."

20

OUR semi-bucolic existence in Hackettsville was interrupted a few times by my being summoned back to Hollywood to write added scenes for *The Devil and the Hot Virgin*. These Hollywood rewrite and revise sessions seldom lasted more than a week and did little to improve the monstrosity we had created, but it gave Johnny Blackwell, Sue Ann Morgan, Marty Goodfellow and everybody else connected with the picture a sense of having done their very best. Their very best, confided my writer buddy, Marve Froman, was hardly the stuff with which empires were built.

"This is a piece of shit," Marve said. "When are those dumb bastards gonna recognize this fact? Why the hell all this rewriting? Christ! I wanna see my wife and girls once in a while." Marve, when he referred to girls, wasn't speaking of his daughters. He meant girls around Hollywood. I have no way of verifying this, but I'm sure Marve has slept with everything female from the rock-ribbed hills of Burbank to the sunny shores of Santa Monica. With him, writing was just an annoying sideline with which he earned enough money for gasoline and oil and medical checkups.

But Marve was right. I thought *The Devil and the Hot Virgin* was positively the worst film I had ever seen, and everybody at the sneak previews they sneaked in sneaky places like Westwood and Pismo Beach and La Jolla booed the picture from the first five minutes on. Once at a drive-in theater in Sacramento the whole audience turned on their bright lights and blew their horns for the entire one hour and thirty-five minutes.

Hells Angels members living in that area cranked up their cycles and zoomed over—they thought they were missing a good old-fashioned gang rape and were terribly disappointed, so they burned down the hamburger stand and lynched the manager. The audience thought this was part of the companion feature and stayed on to see it again.

Nevertheless, all the idiots in command insisted we had a sleeper like *Easy Rider.* After a while their blind faith got to me. Maybe they were right—maybe a few extra scenes, a little judicious editing, and a few minor changes like putting the first half last and the last half first might make the difference between disaster and triumph. After all, as Marty Goodfellow said (something valid, at last), if *Hello Dolly,* the "most God-awful show of all time, with a plagiarized title song and the most cornball production of the ages, can last for eight or nine years on Broadway, *anything* could stand a chance." He was right in every way except one: *The Devil and the Hot Virgin* didn't have David Merrick to defend it.

After the last Hollywood trek, before I left, I said, "I'm not coming back here anymore."

"But you have to," Marty Goodfellow said, with his particular brand of cavalier snideness which he reserved for writers and other scum, "if we want you to. Don't forget, no comeback, no percentage."

"Mr. Goodfellow," I said, using my particular brand of cavalier snideness reserved for personal managers and other vermin, "may I remind you that the contract reads 'reasonable rewrite' and so far we're way the hell past any reasonable rewriting. Christ, we're doing a sequel to this whole horrible mess."

"Yeah," Marve said, "we've written about seven great motion pictures for one lousy piece of shit."

"A piece of shit that's going to make us all rich," shouted Marty, twisting his star sapphire ring to steady his nerves.

"I don't think," Sue Ann Morgan said, "this is any way to speak of a work of art."

"Even a piece of shit can be a work of art," Frederico Fellucio said, "if it's made in Italy."

"Hear! Hear!" Marve said.

"I think I'll go back to Italy," Fellucio said.

"You can't go back till our picture is finished!" Marty Goodfellow almost shouted, twisting his finger along with his star sapphire ring.

"Your picture was finished before it was started," Fellucio said.

Marty's sapphire ring finger was turning black.

"What will you do in Italy?" Marve wanted to know. "There's so many Italians there."

"I'll make wop pictures," Fellucio said.

"I can speak Italian," Sue Ann Morgan said, purring.

"You gotta stay here and finish this picture, too!" Marty screamed at Sue Ann. "Before Johnny gave you your big chance in this movie, you were nothing but a—a—a—"

"Doxy," supplied Marve.

"Yeah," Marty said, "you were nothing but a—what the hell's a doxy?"

"The literal translation is 'beggar's mistress,' but that's become archaic," Marve said.

Marty forgot about Sue Ann for a moment and stared at Marve, then he said in a very hard tone, "Marve, you talk shit!"

"In television movies, we call it dialogue," Marve said serenely. No matter what, Marve was always serene. That's why he could say the most outrageous things to his employers and his tone would imply he meant only the utmost goodwill.

"That's what's wrong with this goddamn *Devil and the Hot Virgin*," Marty yelled, his voice cracking on the high notes. "We need dialogue!"

"The Virgin is supposed to be a deaf-mute," Marve said. "You want dialogue there?"

"That's an idea," Fellucio said. "The Virgin could have an operation which restores her speech."

"Yeah," Marve agreed, "but she still can't hear, so when the phone rings in the bedroom scene, she and the priest just lay there in bed and pay no attention to it."

"What bed?" Marty said. "What priest?"

"*He's* deaf, too," Fellucio said, "or he'd answer the phone and find out that the Pope just fired him."

"What the hell are you talking about?" Marty said, with the attitude now of a whipped dog. "That's not in *The Devil and the Hot Virgin*—there's no bedroom scene in the whole movie."

"Maybe that's what's wrong with it," Marve said.

"I speak Italian," Sue Ann said.

"I can see it all now," Fellucio said to Sue Ann, his manner suddenly becoming ethereal and vaporous. "It's springtime in Naples, and you, Miss Morgan, you are in bed with this deaf man of the cloth—he is listening to your confession—"

"Look, you wop bastard," Marty said, "she stays here till *this* goddamn movie is finished and that's that!"

"Who you calling a wop bastard?" Fellucio said, grabbing Marty Goodfellow by the throat.

"This oughtta be in the picture," Marve said, "right after the scene where the Devil promises the Hot Virgin a million dollars for her soul and her colored television set—"

"Shut up," Fellucio snarled at Marve.

"Anything you say, you wop bastard," Marve said in his quiet way.

"Where were we?" Fellucio said, releasing Marty's red throat.

"You were gonna kill Marty," I said.

"I don't know what it is," Marty said, rubbing his throat and twisting his star sapphire at the same time. "All you people wanted to make this movie with Johnny. Now you all want to leave—before it is finished."

"Look," Marve said, "why don't you preview it a few more times, then take it to one of the networks. They'll buy it—and that will be that."

"You think it's good enough for the networks?" Marty said unbelievingly.

"It's too good," Marve said. "That's why you might have a little trouble, but be firm—you can sell it, Marty."

"What if they don't buy it?" Marty said, big red tears welling up in his bloodshot eyes. "It was made especially for television."

"What's to worry about?" Marve said. "There's always radio."

21

OUR return to Lost Lake was unexpected, by *me*. I thought we were thoroughly settled in Hackettsville and would continue to live there for the rest of our days, with Bobby and Timothy able to attend a proper school, and Reiko able to see the lights of her neighbors.

Of course, all the time we were living in this California mountain community, I had continued to agitate for a return to the wilderness of Canada. Everything I did in the way of home improvement at our new Hackettsville house, I felt I was doing for someone else, which of course is what we are *all* doing. I don't know why Du Pont or Union Carbide can't figure out a way you *can* take it with you. I just hated the idea of someone else luxuriating in our lovely sunken avocado-green bathtub, with the picture-window view of the lush Peach Valley farm country, dusty at dawn and dirty at sundown.

I don't know whether the not-so-veiled remarks I tossed out at Reiko during our residence in the foothills of the Sierra did the trick or not, but they certainly must have had a cumulative effect. How could anyone not be influenced by remarks like: "You certainly don't see many moose around here, do you?" Or "I thought I heard a loon today, but I know it's just my mind playing tricks." Or "Remember how lovely and quiet and peaceful it was at Lost Lake?" And, "Wasn't Bobby cute pulling in those big bass right off our own dock?" Also I added as a real tearjerker, "Isn't it too bad that little Timothy will never know what it was like to live in Canada—in a beautiful log cabin, on an island, surrounded by that lovely clean water and millions of beautiful trees, with no smog, no motorcycle gangs, no bank burnings, and no chance of getting drafted."

"I don't think they'll draft you," Reiko said.

Suddenly I was Nathan Hale. "Why not?" I said.

"You're too nasty," she said. This wasn't the answer I expected.

"That's the idea," I said, recovering. "They *want* nasty soldiers—if you're nice you're liable to get killed."

Immediately Reiko had her arms around me, holding me very tightly. "Oh, Jack-san!" she said.

"Of course," I said, taking advantage of my advantage, "if I get killed on the field of honor, I'll get a nice military funeral."

"Huh?" Reiko said.

"A military funeral," I said. "They're very impressive. My mortal remains will be carried on a flag-draped caisson, with my favorite horse, empty-saddled, following behind."

"You mean," Reiko said, practical now, "we have to buy a horse if you get a military funeral?"

"Look," I said, seeing that our little tableau was getting out of hand, "they're not going to draft me. They wouldn't draft me if the enemy was marching up Hollywood Boulevard. I was thinking of Bobby and Timothy."

This shook Reiko up pretty well because she had mentioned her trepidation a few times before. Although Bobby was only eight years old and Timothy had just about arrived at two.

Reiko, with typical Oriental fatalistic reasoning, had them both being drafted and sent to Vietnam to join up with the 1st Air Cavalry, or, worse yet, being shipped to Arizona to fight the Apaches. I tried to make it clear that the Apaches, although they were still mad at the white man, didn't fight anymore; they made pots, which they sold to tourists, which immediately crumbled upon getting them home, giving the Apaches a lick of retribution.

Reiko would not accept this simple truth. She insisted the Indians were out there somewhere. At the ready. She might be right.

I don't think that anything I said had anything to do

with Reiko's decision to once again leave the comfort and the imagined safety of civilization for the rigors and precarious existence deep in the wilderness of northern Ontario. And it had to be her decision because by the time it came, I had given up. I had resigned myself to the dull routine of small-town living. Which I liked very much, but I knew that it was challenge and curiosity that kept you young. Funny—I was curious as hell and also I was being challenged by every credit card company in America, but my hair got grayer every day. But, on the other hand, I still had all the hair I started with fifty-six years ago, which may or may not be anchored into my scalp by challenge or curiosity. I must ask my barber about this. Reiko is my barber, so I may not learn too much. Or she'll give me an answer like: "Make love makes strong hair." Which, translated, means, "Early to bed, late to rise, and you'll have ringlets down to your thighs," in Japanese.

The first inkling I had of Reiko's disenchantment with living in Hackettsville was when she started complaining about just about everything. Mr. McCurdy, the garbage man, charged too much money. This was true, but Mr. McCurdy had a monopoly in Hackettsville and a secret dump, which was as mysterious as an elephant's graveyard—nobody could ever find it. Mr. McCurdy also had a nice way with statements. Across the top of every bill, which had to be paid three months *in advance,* he had stamped, "Avoid Legal Action—pay this bill now." I never could figure out what the hell legal action this oaf had in mind, but I'm sure it frightened the timorous into paying their garbage bills the day they received them. I held out a little—I paid only two months in advance. No garbage jockey was going to intimidate *me!*

Reiko grumbled about having to go to the grocery store so often because she always forgot some small item, like bread, or milk, or meat, or dog biscuits.

"Make a list!" I screamed at her four or five times a day. "Every housewife makes a list of what she needs at the store, then she doesn't forget when she gets there!"

"I don't forget when I get there," Reiko said. "I forget here—before I leave to go to the store."

"How could you forget dog biscuits?" I said. "We got two dogs and a wolf—what the hell do you think they eat?"

"What about Pussycat?" was Reiko's illogical retort.

"Cougars don't eat dog biscuits—" I said.

"They eat elk," Bobby said.

"They don't have elk at Jerry's Market," Reiko said.

"What about the A&P?" I said, complicating matters for myself.

"They also eat mice and gophers," Bobby said.

"They got mice at Jerry's Market," Reiko said.

"In boxes or cans?" I said.

"No, running around the floor—that's why Jerry got that cat," she said.

"Why didn't he get a cougar?" Bobby said.

"Jerry's too nervous," Reiko said, "and he's afraid of cougars. He's also afraid of cats."

"He must lead a pretty miserable existence," I said. "If he's afraid of cats, how does he live with a cat in his store?"

"He pretends it's a mouse," Reiko said.

"I like mice," Bobby said.

"Good," I said. "That's what we're having for dinner tonight—mouse burgers and soy sauce."

"We're having spaghetti," Reiko said.

"We always have spaghetti," Bobby said.

"Or rice," I said.

"I'm going back to Japan," Reiko said. "Give me my money."

Every time she threatens to go back to Japan, or I threaten to go to Tahiti and drink, she says, "Give me my money." What money, I have never been able to find out. Maybe she means her share of what we make on the Griffin, Carson, Mike Douglas and other talk shows, which I always throw into the common pot which is meant for all of us—Reiko, me, Bobby and Timothy. This money we spend on all nonessentials like food, lights, fuel oil, laundry and dry cleaning. If there's anything left over, we buy New York State Lottery tickets from my Buffalo brother. I don't think they've ever let any California resident win, but it's the only game in town. Winning the million-dollar grand prize would make us better people, I'm sure. Or at least it would help us live (after taxes) graciously—for a few weeks, anyway. I don't know why they don't have a New York State Lottery with New York State as the grand prize—maybe some mental patient would win it, and take it over and run it *his* way. It would be interesting to see how long it would be before the improvement would be noticed.

Another slight sign of restlessness, or maybe longing, that I detected in Reiko was when a long V line of Canada geese flew over, flying north. Reiko always stopped whatever she was doing and watched them until they were long out of sight over the distant blue hills, then she would almost sigh and return to her Hackettsville routine, which that spring entailed the building of a bar in the corner of our living room. Neither one of us drinks, but we felt we couldn't live without our very own bar— and in case Reiko forgot she was a hermitess and invited someone up to our hilltop home, we would be prepared to give being the perfect host and hostess a whirl, although I doubt the success of this because we had long ago abandoned any attempt at being the Jackie and Ari of the outboard motor set.

If by some miracle we did give a party and one of our invited guests spoke Swahili, we might interpret it as old Brookville or Old Westbury. We were that unaccustomed to the human race.

But this was living a dream—I was sure we'd never have anyone up. Everything we were creating on top of that hill was in anticipation of some great social gathering that was never to be, but we always spoke as if we were expecting a social season which would make January and February in Palm Beach or August in Saratoga look like a Jehovah's Witness convention in downtown Traverse City, Michigan. We always, as we moved the furniture around, said things like: "Some people can sit here, and we can put a couple of ashtrays on this table here" or "If they want to get close to the fire, they can sit here" or "This would make a nice little conversation nook here" or "People can serve themselves from the buffet here and sit over there, and we must remember to order some paper guest towels with our initials on them." We were playing Grand Hotel, there's no doubt about it. We would *never* have anyone standing around our bar, unless it was the man from the bank wondering where the hell the last three mortgage payments were. Then I would also be standing at the bar, matching him drink for drink—also wondering where the hell the last three mortgage payments were.

We lived as the great plantation owners of the South lived after the Civil War, planning mythical galas which we both knew were viewy-dewy-eyed to a ridiculous degree. But this situation wasn't sad like the scene of an old madame, with a parlor full of middle-aged poules de Beauty Rest, outside an abandoned army base, sitting around waiting for the action that has long since gone. Reiko and I knew we were playing a fun game and didn't really give a damn if the only guests at our soirees were just us. This sounds like we don't like people, which isn't the case; we were content with each other.

I think the two incidents which decided Reiko that we should forget about Hackettsville and head north were, one, the raccoon hunter, and, two, the airport bus.

The raccoon hunter was equipped with two hounds of hell who seemed to be wired up to stereo speakers, and when they started their unearthly baying at midnight might just have well been in the bedroom with us. The hunter, whom, we found out, had been hunting in these parts since the great glacier had retreated, seemed to think that this gave him priority over the rights and comforts of anyone else. Things had changed since the Ice Age, and there were a few people now living within his hunting preserve, which was now owned by these few people. Which, of course, he did not acknowledge.

The raccoon hunter wore a carbide light in his cap, which I'm sure was used to blind Cyclops' other eye. It was that bright. His armament apparently consisted of mortars, rockets and bazookas, from the sound of it. This coon hunter could have stopped a Sherman tank attack. I don't know how many raccoons he wiped out, but the deer population dwindled considerably. This sportsman "jack-lighted" deer. That is, his hounds scared up the deer and ran them within range of his powerful light, where they would stand blinded and trembling with fear until he blasted them to death with his shotgun. This butchery, so close to home, sickened Reiko.

The airport bus was something else. Late one afternoon, as I was picking up stones (a lifetime occupation in Peach Valley) and dumping them into a depressed area in our front lawn, the airport bus drove into our driveway and right across our lovely Kentucky blue crabgrass, and almost up to our front door, knocking down a Japanese stone lantern in the process.

What the hell now? I thought, as a short man with large thick glasses, magnifying his mole eyes, climbed out of the bus and walked over to me, with a limp white hand extended in a gesture of slimy friendship. I took his hand, expecting to pull back a subpoena announcing a suit brought by some airport bus line I had defrauded in my nonopulent youth, but his hand was empty, although a bit mossy.

"My name is Kingley Wright," he said. "I brought some of the boys over to see where Jack Douglas lives."

"Oh," I said, glancing toward the busload he had driven up to our preserve. The "boys" were an ominous-looking group with not a forehead among them.

"Which Jack Douglas were you looking for?" I asked. "Jack Douglas, the Greek Hollywood travel film producer? He lives in Hollywood."

"No," Mr. Myopic said, "Jack Douglas, the famous writer and television personality, and his lovely wife, Reiko."

"Oh, yeah," I said. "They moved. They went back to the city. They couldn't stand the noise of all those horny crickets every night. Did you ever know how they do it? The crickets, I mean?"

"How the crickets do *what?*"

"Hump," I said. "Crickets hump by rubbing their hind legs together. And they can do it all night long. And that's what happened to Jack Douglas and his lovely wife, Reiko—the cricket humpers drove them out."

"I've never heard of anyone humping a cricket," Mr. Myopic said, missing the point entirely. "Woolly caterpillars, maybe, but crickets—I dunno."

"Well," I said, "I've enjoyed this little nature talk but I've got to feed my Siberian tiger now. It's almost five o'clock, and if I don't give him a live steer by five o'clock on the nose, he rips his Siberian tiger cage all to hell—and they're expensive." I was saying anything now because I felt as if I were conversing with a man with a head full of broken toys. A moment later I found out how on target I was.

"The boys here," the man said, again indicating the airport bus full of shadowy faces, "are from the Dingman State Hospital, up near Bakersfield way."

"Isn't that a mental institution?" I asked.

"Yes," the man said, "they watch Jack Douglas and his lovely wife, Reiko, all the time on the TV and they wanted to see where they lived. Jack Douglas and his lovely wife, Reiko, are their favorites."

"Maybe I better say hello to them," I said, walking toward the airport bus.

"Bully," Mr. Kingley Wright said. "You are a good sort."

"Yeah," I said.

The men in the bus showed no sign of recognition when I stuck my head in the window. "Hi ya, fellers," I said.

No one answered or even looked directly at me. "This is Jack Douglas, fellers," Mr. Wright said. "You watch him and his lovely wife, Reiko, on television all the time."

Nobody seemed to care.

"It takes them awhile," Mr. Wright said.

"To do what?" I said.

"To warm up to strangers," Mr. Wright said.

"But I'm not a stranger," I said. "They watch me and my lovely wife, Reiko, all the time on television."

Mr. Wright looked at me strangely. Momentarily, I thought I was going to be invited to ride on the bus.

"Well," Mr. Wright said, extending his droopy hand again, "it's been a pleasure, Mr. Douglas, and I'm sure all the fellers got a big kick out of meeting you."

Mr. Wright got behind the wheel and started the bus' engine, and as he backed up, to swing out of our driveway, I heard one of the fellers say, "Where the hell are we goin'? I thought we were gonna get out and take a leak?"

Mr. Wright gunned the engine and they were gone. Golly, I thought to myself, wasn't it nice of Mr. Wright to drive that busload of nuts all the way up to Peach Valley to meet Jack Douglas and his lovely wife, Reiko, and to take a leak—not necessarily in that order.

After the funny farm group left, Reiko came bursting out of the front door in a new pants suit outfit and completely made up for pictures. She thought the airport bus was part of a *House Beautiful* tour, and she fell apart when I told her what it was. One of the things she sobbed was that she had had enough, and she'd rather live in a place where you could be eaten by a bear than visited by a busload of mental patients. This kind of thing does not upset me, but I said nothing.

One week later Charlie Burke taxied his Cessna 180 up to our airplane dock at Lost Lake. We were home.

22

THE rest of the world had changed, but Lost Lake remained the same. The first evening of our return, I walked a couple of miles through the woods bordering the shoreline and climbed to the top of an immense rock on a point of land jutting into the lake, which was known as Lovers' Leap—why, I don't know. I would have thought if a pair of lovers had some sort of a problem which Ann Landers or Dear Abby found unsolvable, they would have not journeyed 116 miles back into the bush to find a rock to leap off. They could join hands and jump off the top of the Chinookville Hilton, which, although it is only two stories high, would, I'm sure, have accomplished the same result. And if they changed their minds halfway down (as sometimes happens), they would be much nearer an emergency medical center. Or a filling station, complete with free glasses and Band-Aids. If, on the other hand, they decided against doing what they were doing— halfway down from Lovers' Leap, 116 miles back in the bush—they might not be found for several years. By that time Ann Landers and Dear Abby might have completely forgotten their problem, what with the plethora of unwed mothers (since the last General Motors' strike) pestering hell out of them.

This whole thing brings up a question: Why hasn't some enterprising organization like the Holiday Inn people constructed a chain of Lovers' Leaps all over the country— and in more convenient locations? A really progressive inn could feature honeymoon suites *and* Lovers' Leaps—then if things didn't work out that first night. . . .

I sat high up on the promontory of our Lovers' Leap,

enjoying the glassy smoothness of the lake and the eerie shrills of the loons calling to each other across the now-blackening water. A lone beaver swam silently from the north end of the lake, where an enormous ancient beaver dam slowed the waters flowing into the snakelike Lost River, which led after many tortuous, rapids-plagued miles to Moose Lake. The beaver was on his way to a particularly succulent grove of aspens at the south end. This was a good four-mile swim, but apparently he thought the effort worth it. Sometimes beavers will haul heavy alder limbs the entire length of the lake to make repairs on their dam, which gives credence to the Cherokee Indians' theory that the earth was constructed with the assistance of beavers. This sounds quite logical. God must have had *some* help. The unions would have insisted.

As I watched this beaver swimming toward an evening of quiet feasting, I thought of all the Hollywood beavers busily trying to dam up their little streams of thought into ponds of gold, complete with a cabana and dolphins.

To sit high on a rocky ledge overlooking a beautiful Canadian lake, in the softly creeping twilight, is very conducive to objective thought. Objective and pleasant. All the rough edges of life are smoothed away and disappear into the timeless mistings of the cool dusk. It is the hour to look back and try to remember what you did right. I never could recall *anything*. The things I had done wrong since I got off Pablum were revived with no effort at all. Sorting them out was the problem—from the small boo-boos to the ghastly errors, there were thousands of situations I had handled badly—but, as I said on my high perch overlooking lovely Lost Lake, these misadventures and mistakes were as nothing. And in actuality this was true. Why anyone goes through life struggling to achieve some impossible goal is folly at its peak. One should try to get through life with the greatest amount of pleasure and the least effort. Ask anybody on welfare.

From my position on the point of land, I was on the opposite side of a small bay, across from our tiny main island. The lamps in the living room of the lodge were making darting shafts of yellow light across the deep black purple as a slight breeze riffled the water, and I could smell the birch logs burning in the fireplace. The aroma reminded me of California. I pictured the barbecue pits were being readied for the thousands of backyard Bacchanalia, which was part of the magic of California. Half-cooked hamburgers, frizzled hot dogs, and Adolf's Meat Tenderizer were a way of life in the Golden State.

It gave me a nice warm glow to realize what I had given up. Of my own free will, I had said good-bye to Hollywood and Vine, Laura La Plante Boulevard, Lola Lane, and the Avenue of the Stars, the Farmers' Market, the Century Plaza Hotel, and the 80-foot-high HOLLYWOOD sign, which is high in the hills overlooking Glendale, the home of Forest Lawn, the Disneyland of Death.

Without a shred of remorse I left the horrible "dailiness" of a fiery sun filtered through a cloud of poison gas, which prompted hourly official warning bulletins concerning the folly of breathing. I left the miles of broad Beverly Hills boulevards lined with stately royal palms, which, instead of nests of robins, had colonies of bubonic rats in their hair and reached their leafy arms to pray all the live-long day for the exterminator.

With nary a pang, I had turned my back on Palm Springs, the Coney Island of the West, with its tramway to nowhere, its endless parade of star-named golf tourneys, its sun-seared females, who were convinced that a greasy Cordovan leather face was the most attractive possession a woman could have.

I had said good-bye to the glamorous, shoeshine parlor openings, the movie theater closings and the acres of foot fungus on the Sunset Strip.

It was hail and farewell to all of those superstars of today: Mary Lou Tiger, who clawed her way to the top in *The Hooker and the Machine,* the story of a computer-run whorehouse. (It was like *The Dating Game* without the suspense of guessing the outcome.) Inger Fauss and Peer Aulberg in *I, a Woman, Part 47* (this is apparently catching on as a series); Gilbert Sashimi, the Japanese Mick Jagger, who, as the Tokyo *Times* critic put it, is outrageously kinky in a Hong Kong remake of *Gone with the Wind*. Gilbert Sashimi, is not—repeat, is *not*—engaged to Hugh O'Brian, as suggested in Ed Sullivan's Friday column. He's happily married to Sessue Hayakawa's nephew, Randy Schwartz. (This was in Sullivan's Monday column.) Gentle Ben Morganstern, the star of *Bestiality*, the story of a horny boy and his dog. Barbra Tittinghill who thought Andre Previn was serious until Mia had her twins, but who carried bravely on to become one of England's greatest Hamlets (she played it in the nude, with a Roman candle instead of a costar). I'll never see any of these devastatingly attractive people again, which, somehow, high on my lovely rock, with an enormous full moon rising over the eastern edge of the Stygian forest and the sounds of the Canadian wilderness around me—the deep-throated frogs, the far-off owls calling to each other, and the loons, much softer now, answering the owls—gave me an inner glow of the satisfaction of doing something right, for maybe the first time in my life.

When I arrived back at the lodge, after a precarious (without a flashlight) walk around the little bay, Reiko said someone had called, she didn't know who. This was typical of Reiko's messages to me. I've always felt that it would have been better not to mention anyone calling. That way, I wouldn't have to wonder for the rest of my life who the hell called at 8:15 P.M. on Tuesday, June 18th, 1970.

Also, I reasoned, who *would* call? Nobody knew we were here.

At 10 P.M. Irving Laveeeene had me on the phone:

"They *love* you!!!!" These were his first words.

"How did you know I was here?" These were my first words.

"They really love you," Irving said.

"All right," I said, giving up, "who loves me?"

"Everybody. Johnny Blackwell loves you. Fellucio loves you. Marty Goodfellow loves you—"

"How about Sue Ann Morgan?" I said.

"She's promised you a good hump," Irving said.

"Why me?" I said. "I'm only a writer."

"She figures that someday you may be a producer," Irving said.

"She's sweet," I said.

"They figure the movie's gonna be a smash," Irving said.

"What about the last scene where Sue Ann's got Johnny and the Devil by the balls?" I said.

"Everybody's talking about it," Irving said.

"I wonder why?" I said.

"How soon can you get out here?" Irving said, switching to his businessman's tone.

"Out where?" I said, knowing perfectly well.

"Out where the big money is—Hollywood," Irving said, I thought, with reverence.

"I just got home," I said. "You should be here, Irving. The biggest moon you've ever seen is just coming over the pines, and the lake is like a huge rippled mirror."

"Jesus H. Christ!" Irving said. "I've been up there in that goddamn wilderness with you. Remember? I almost went nuts!"

"But you were starting to relax," I said. "A couple of more days and you would have been completely cured."

"Completely cured? Of what?" he said. "My sanity? Look, schmuck—"

"Don't use any dirty Yiddish on me just to make a point," I said.

"Don't you want to be a success?" he said. "Don't you want to be the biggest man in Hollywood?"

"Yes," I said, "but I want to do it like Howard Hughes does it—by remote control. Very remote and very controlled."

"Jesus, what a tourist *you* are!" Irving said. "There *is* no Howard Hughes!"

"Who's that guy who used to live like a hermit on the top floor of that Las Vegas hotel?"

"God," Irving said, "just God."

"Oh," said I, with an uncomfortable feeling that Irving Laveeeene might be onto something.

"Whaddya say?" Irving said. "Hop a plane and get your ass out here and live a little. There's a fortune in it." Then he mentioned a money figure, and he was right. There *was* a fortune in it. Not a fortune which could be mentioned in the same breath with Josephine, the plumber's, but a fortune enough for a former sixth grade president of the East Rockaway Grammar School.

"Who knows?" Irving bubbled on. "In a couple of years, with a little help from your friends, you could be the biggest man in Hollywood."

At that moment a wolf howled somewhere far off in the bush, and our wolf answered him. It was a lonely, mournful sound, with all the sorrows of the world commingled within its low tonal range. It was wild, lost, and despairing but it was beautiful. Quietly, I replaced the phone on its cradle. It didn't ring again.

Two months later, as the early morning sky was turning pink, I walked out to my rocky point and sat down to enjoy the lovely beginning of a new day.

Just as the sun shot its first rays through the lake mists, I heard the hum of an approaching plane, and in a few moments I saw it. The plane belonged to the Ontario Geological Survey. After landing, they taxied into the small bay between our camp and me, and bumped into the shore about halfway. The two Geological Survey men, who had probed the area for the five years since we bought our wilderness home, jumped down from the cockpit and tied the plane to two birches at the water's edge, placing bumpers along the pontoons so they wouldn't be damaged, then they immediately disappeared into the bush.

Casually, because I had seen them so many times before, I wondered what brought them down so early in the morning. I was to know all too soon.

As I sat there daydreaming about nothing and enjoying the cool, crisp September morning with its promise of a good day, I was not conscious of a new sound. The sound which was more of a drone. The drone of millions of black flies, which is not uncommon in this part of the world. The noise grew louder. And louder. —And *louder!* Suddenly over the trees at the north end of the lake, what seemed like a fleet of helicopters—*giant* helicopters—appeared. The racket became unbearable as these enormous choppers got closer.

Dangling from beneath each machine was a huge piece of equipment. There were gargantuan earth-moving machines hung by thick cables from beneath the helicopters, their giant steel jaws and claws open and ready—looking like angry prehistoric monsters. There were huge platforms swinging under the roaring blades—platforms stacked high with hundreds of cases of high explosives. There were drills as big around as redwoods, and there were huge generators and pumps, and platoons of hard-hatted men packed like cattle in enclosed cars beneath these airborne monstrosities. I couldn't believe what I was seeing until they started to land one by one in a large piece of open ground in back of our little cove. I didn't realize what the hell it was all about until I saw the large insignia printed on the side of one of the giant helicopters: INTERNATIONAL NICKEL COMPANY.

Be sure and watch for my new release from Hollywood, *The Devil and International Nickel*. It's Sue Ann Morgan's best effort to date—she balls the United Mine Workers.